*Structure and functions
of rural workers' organisations*

Structure and functions of rural workers' organisations

A workers' education manual

International Labour Office   Geneva

ISBN 92-2-101839-3

First published 1978

ILO publications can be obtained through major booksellers or ILO local offices in many countries, or direct from ILO Publications, International Labour Office, CH-1211 Geneva 22, Switzerland. A catalogue or list of new publications will be sent free of charge from the above address.

Printed by Atar S.A., Geneva, Switzerland

Preface

The majority of the world's poor are rural workers, whether they be wage earners, self-employed subsistence owner-occupiers or landless labourers. It is now becoming increasingly recognised that the improvement of the conditions of life and work of these millions of workers is in large measure dependent upon the extent to which they can be mobilised—both to help themselves and to contribute to national development.

This was one of the reasons underlying the adoption by the International Labour Conference in June 1975 of a Convention and a Recommendation concerning Organisations of Rural Workers and Their Role in Economic and Social Development. These instruments defined the term "rural workers", affirmed the right of them all (both employed and self-employed) to freedom of association, set out the conditions necessary for the development of their organisations, outlined the roles that they might undertake and suggested ways and means by which their development might be furthered.

However, there is a world of difference between agreeing that certain aims are desirable and actually achieving those aims. This publication is intended to help towards bridging that gap in so far as rural workers' organisations are concerned.

One of the principal means of helping workers' organisations to develop and grow strong is education—workers' education. Education is, in fact, among the main issues dealt with in the two instruments referred to above. However, whilst there is a wealth of workers' education material available, it is almost entirely concerned with the needs and circumstances of urban workers. It is for this reason that, in continuation of a long tradition of service to workers' education, the ILO has produced this publication especially to meet the needs of the rural sector.

It may be said that those who are convinced of the need to develop and strengthen organisations of rural workers fall into one of two broad categories: those who are anxious to make a contribution to that end but who do not feel that they have sufficient background to do so; and those who are already involved in the activity but who feel that they need wider background

V

knowledge concerning the nature and methods of work of rural workers' organisations in other countries and in other parts of the world.

This book can help to meet the needs of both these groups. For the former, it provides background material on the various categories of rural worker, the development of rural workers' organisations, why they organise, how their organisations are built and what they actually do or can do. For those in the latter group, whether they be from other workers' organisations or from the rural workers' organisations themselves, it provides both comparative and specific information on what is actually being done, in the developing world in particular, by rural workers who are already organised. It pays special attention to the two critical factors: the importance of ensuring as sound a financial base as possible; and the importance of developing services to meet the needs of members. Whilst it is not a textbook, it is so designed that it may be used as a basis for practical workers' education work, particularly the kind of work intended for the development of both local and national leadership.

The presentation—the original text of which was prepared for the ILO by Mr. Edward M. Colbert, a lifelong trade unionist with many years of practical experience with rural workers' organisations in developing countries—is based on actual cases, problems and activities. The approach turns on two essential themes: that without organisation the rural worker is back to "the feeble strength of one"; and that a workers' organisation exists only to "further and defend the interests of its members". It provides down-to-earth general and detailed information and guidance for those who wish to make a practical contribution towards assisting rural workers to organise and so to improve their lot.

Note. Whenever money matters have been referred to in the text the amounts involved have been given in NUs—national units of currency. The figures used are the actual figures for the national currency: for example, if the African union mentioned on p. 48 had been in Senegal, the figures quoted would have been in CFA francs. Thus it is important to appreciate that whilst the NUs are constant and comparable within each country, they are not comparable between one country and another.

The main reason for this method of presentation is to discourage the reader from making comparisons with his own or an international currency and with his own standards of income and living. Comparisons of incomes are meaningless without a full knowledge of the respective costs of living, the spending habits of national and local cultures, the number of hours worked to earn the income, deductions from pay, taxation and (in some countries) additions to incomes from social security funds. It can be taken for granted that the incomes of the members in each country for which values are given in NUs are markedly less than the national average, and in almost all cases are also markedly less than the incomes of industrial workers in the country concerned.

Contents

Part III. Servicing the interests of rural workers

Part IV. Conclusion

Appendices

Photographs

The International Labour Office wishes to make acknowledgement to the following for permission to reproduce photographs: the National Union of Agricultural and Allied Workers, London (facing p. 16, above); the National Union of Agricultural and Allied Workers, London and Spencer's Pictorial Press, Grimsby (facing p. 16, below); D. Hodsdon, Esq. (facing p. 94, below). All the other photographs are taken from the ILO Photo Library, Geneva.

Part I

The historical and legal background

Rural workers

1

Who are they?

Rural workers, first and foremost, are "workers": that is, they obtain food, shelter and clothing for themselves and their families by their toil. By "rural worker" we mean any person engaged in agriculture or a related occupation in a rural area, whether as a wage earner or as a self-employed person.[1]

Wage earners in the rural sector include all permanent, seasonal and temporary or casual workers employed for wages in agriculture and related occupations: many of these, especially those whose employment is temporary or seasonal, may also be migrant workers.

The self-employed group includes such persons as sharecroppers, tenants, small owner-occupiers, squatters and nomads. Tenants, sharecroppers and similar categories of agricultural worker pay a landlord for the use of the land. The payment may take the form of a fixed rent in cash, in kind, in labour or in a combination of these; or it may be a rent in kind consisting of an agreed share of the produce; or the tenant or sharecropper may be remunerated by a share of the produce.

Small owner-occupiers are cultivators of individually held or communally held land who derive their main income from agriculture, by working the land either themselves or with the help only of their families or of occasional outside labour. On the other hand, those who permanently employ workers or employ a substantial number of seasonal workers or have any land cultivated by sharecroppers or tenants are not themselves considered to be rural workers.

Landless labourers are those who live in rural areas and who have no access to land to cultivate (through either ownership, tenancy or common usage) and who therefore depend for their livelihood on hiring out their labour for wages. In practice, the term may also be considered to include those who have access only to a plot of land that is too small to support them and

---

[1] The full internationally agreed definition of a rural worker is set out in the ILO Rural Workers' Organisations Convention, 1975 (No. 141); see Appendix B.

their family. The rural unemployed—those who would be independent cultivators if they could find land to work, or who would be wage earners if they could find employment—may also be looked upon as landless labourers.

Special mention must be made of "family workers", generally the wife and children of the rural worker, who often work beside him, or in his place where there is an extensive migration of male workers seeking employment, or where the accepted tradition is that the woman supervises the cultivation of the small farm plot while the husband works elsewhere. In some countries there are many rural women workers, especially in the self-employed and casually employed groups.

These categories of rural worker often overlap. The same worker may belong to two or more categories at the same time or over the course of the year. For example, a rural worker may own a small plot of land or be a sharecropper on a small plot and also work as a wage earner on a seasonal or casual basis.

How many rural workers are there?

Over two-thirds of the world's population lives in rural areas. Although, in Western Europe, only between 3 and 19 per cent of the labour force is engaged in agriculture, the proportion is much greater elsewhere: between 40 and 60 per cent in Latin America, between 60 and 80 per cent in most Asian countries and between 60 and 90 per cent in most parts of Africa.

In most developed and developing countries wage earners form a minority among rural workers, the majority of whom are in the non-wage-earning category.

In 11 developed countries of Western Europe (Austria, Belgium, Denmark, France, Federal Republic of Germany, Italy, Netherlands, Norway, Sweden, Switzerland, United Kingdom) the percentage of wage earners among the total agricultural labour force varies between 55 (United Kingdom) and 7.6 (Belgium). In the USSR this percentage is 17, while in six other Eastern European countries (Bulgaria, Czechoslovakia, Hungary, Poland, Romania, Yugoslavia) it varies between 29 (Czechoslovakia) and 7 (Poland, Yugoslavia). The proportions for Canada and the United States are 28 per cent and 37 per cent respectively.

In 11 countries in Africa (Algeria, Botswana, Egypt, Gabon, Ghana, Ivory Coast, Liberia, Libyan Arab Jamahiriya, Mauritius, Morocco, Sierra Leone) the proportion of wage earners engaged in agriculture exceeds one-half only in Algeria (about 60 per cent) and Mauritius (about 90 per cent). In most of these 11 countries such wage earners represent about 10 per cent (Ghana, Liberia) or between 7 and 0.7 per cent (Gabon, Ivory Coast, Botswana, Sierra Leone, in decreasing order). In Botswana, for example, about 90 per cent of the population are self-employed persons in agriculture.

In the 16 countries in Latin America (Argentina, Brazil, Chile, Colombia,

Costa Rica, Dominican Republic, Ecuador, El Salvador, Honduras, Jamaica, Mexico, Nicaragua, Panama, Peru, Uruguay, Venezuela) for which statistical data are available from 1960 onwards, wage earners represent more than half the total agricultural labour force only in Chile, Costa Rica, El Salvador, Mexico and Uruguay. In the other countries the percentages vary between 48 and 15.5 (Argentina, Nicaragua, Colombia, Jamaica, Ecuador, Venezuela, Peru, Honduras, Brazil, Dominican Republic, Panama—listed in decreasing order).

In 12 countries in Asia (India, Indonesia, Iran, Israel, Jordan, Kuwait, Malaysia, Pakistan, Philippines, Sri Lanka, Syrian Arab Republic, Thailand), only in one (Sri Lanka, in which the economy is based on plantation agriculture) do wage earners represent more than half the total agricultural labour force. In Kuwait wage earners also predominate in agriculture, but in that country as a whole the agricultural labour force represents only 1 per cent of the total labour force. In the other countries mentioned the percentage of wage earners in agriculture varies between 45 in Malaysia and 1.5 in India. [1]

What are their conditions of life and work?

The conditions of the rural workers' lives and work vary greatly between categories and between areas of the world and even within individual countries.

Speaking of rural workers in developing countries, the President of the World Bank has observed:

When we reflect that, of the 2,000 million persons living in our developing member countries, nearly two-thirds—some 1,300 million—are members of farm families, and that of these there are some 900 million whose annual incomes average less than US$100, what frame of reference are we to call on to make that fact meaningful?

To many in the affluent world, to be a farmer suggests a life of dignity and decency, free of the irritation and pollution of modern existence: a life close to nature and rich in satisfactions.

That may be what life on the land ought to be. But for hundreds of millions of these subsistence farmers, life is neither satisfying nor decent. Hunger and malnutrition menace their families. Illiteracy forecloses their futures. Disease and death visit their villages too often, stay too long, and return too soon.

Their nation may be developing, but their lives are not. The miracle of the Green Revolution may have arrived, but for the most part, the poor farmer has not been able to participate in it. He simply cannot afford to pay for the irrigation, the pesticide, the fertiliser—or perhaps even for the land itself on which his title may be vulnerable and his tenancy uncertain.

His nation may have doubled or tripled its educational budget, and in the capital city there may be an impressive university. But for 300 million children of poor farmers like himself there are still no schools—and for hundreds of millions of others if a school, no qualified teacher—and if a qualified teacher, no adequate books.

His nation may be improving its communications, and jet aircraft may be landing at

---

[1] ILO: *Organisations of rural workers and their role in economic and social development*, Report VI(1), International Labour Conference, 59th Session, Geneva, 1974, pp. 8-9.

its international airport in increasing numbers. But for the poor farmer who has seldom seen an airplane, and never an airport, what communications really means—and what he all too often does not have—is a simple all-weather road that would allow him to get his meagre harvest to market when the time is right and the prices are good.

Let us be candid.

What these men want are jobs for their survival, food for their families, and a future for their children. They want the simple satisfaction of working toward something better: toward an end to misery, and a beginning of hope. [1]

The sharecroppers, tenants and similar rural workers in most developing and some developed countries have little or no security of tenure in relation to the land they work; they have no written contracts fixing either an equitable share in the production or an equitable rent, and no provision for an automatic extension of the lease ("tenants at will"—the will of the landlord). The sharecroppers, tenants, squatters and subsistence owner-occupiers lack the means and incentive to increase their production since they are unable to save and invest; and in the case of sharecroppers, even when they are able to buy fertiliser or better seed and do succeed in increasing production, the landlord gets half and more without having risked anything. They also face the risk of drought, flood, hurricane, fire, insects and plant diseases which can mean their being deprived of all means of livelihood and even their death by starvation.

The majority of agricultural wage earners in most developing and in some developed countries are engaged on a seasonal (and often a casual) basis. Most seasonal or casual workers do not receive any form of social security or unemployment benefit, holidays with pay, or sick or maternity leave. Indeed, many permanent rural wage earners lack these same benefits. Wages in rural areas, both in cash terms and in real terms, are generally lower than in the cities, and the hours of work are longer. While in most countries the agricultural wage earner may be covered by general or special labour legislation, the administration of the law is often weak and ineffective.

In most Latin American countries colonial rule ended over 150 years ago; and yet the majority of the rural workers remained subject to a system that has been described as "internal colonialism". Large *haciendas*, [2] taken from the lands which belonged to the indigenous communities, were established or extended. Peasants tried to defend their traditional rights in vain. Some of the violence that has occurred in some countries in this region can be said to have resulted in part from this so-called "culture of repression".

Whilst in a few countries the old patterns are giving way to new and more liberal systems, in most there are still, on the one hand, millions of rural workers who farm—often as tenants or sharecroppers—plots of land *(minifundios)* which are too small to provide themselves and their families

---

[1] Robert S. McNamara: *Address to the Board of Governors* (Washington, DC, World Bank, 25 Sep. 1972), p. 10.

[2] Certain Spanish words are commonly used in connection with land reform in Latin American countries. They include *hacienda* or *latifundio,* a large estate; *latifundia,* the system of large estates; *minifundio,* a small plot of land insufficient to sustain the cultivator and his family; *minifundia,* the system of these small plots of land.

with a decent standard of living; and on the other hand, large estates *(latifundios)* which, because of the extensive methods of cultivation and often because a large proportion of the land is left fallow, do not provide anything like the level of employment opportunities of which they are capable.

The self-employed cannot get more land, and in many cases they are dependent on the will of the landlord for the use of the land they do cultivate. There are virtually no alternative opportunities for them to earn a living in the rural areas. The ties which bind the agricultural worker on the large estates are far more tenacious than those on an industrial worker in a factory. The estate is a kind of self-supporting closed world: whereas the urban worker can change his job without having to move house, the worker on the *latifundio* cannot leave without giving up the land and house he is occupying, and in any case the expense of travelling the large distances involved virtually precludes him from finding another place. Thus, on his own, he has practically no opportunity to change or improve his circumstances; and yet, because the number of people in these rural areas continues to increase (despite the drift to the towns), those circumstances are bound to deteriorate.

In Asia the situation of the rural worker is probably the most complex and "the one in which the problems of underdevelopment exist in perhaps their most acute form. All the economic and social data show that in some of these countries people are living at a level so abysmally low that it can scarcely qualify as 'subsistence'." [1] A very large number of Asian rural workers are landless and able to find only casual employment. Some countries have many small owner-occupiers; there is still a large concentration of land in the hands of a few. And absent landlords and "defective systems of sharecropping and tenancy, often in association with a faulty credit and marketing system, seriously affect peasants' income". [2]

In Sri Lanka, to give but one example, the FAO Special Committee on Agrarian Reform noted "the serious problem of landless peasants and of peasants who possess only extremely small plots. A large majority of the present small tillers are sharecroppers subject to oppressive conditions." [3] This Committee also summarised the immense problem of the rural workers in India by pointing out that "there are 100 million landless peasants and 185 million tillers working on plots with an area of less than 2 hectares; [4] the number of those who seek employment in agriculture and other sectors of the economy is growing rapidly; the agricultural population now exceeds that of 20 years ago by 150 million". [5]

In Africa the entirely different traditional cultures and systems of land ownership, coupled with the effects of colonisation, have produced

---

[1] Xavier Flores: *Agricultural organisations and development* (Geneva, ILO, 1971), p. 423.

[2] FAO: *Report of the Special Committee on Agrarian Reform* (Rome, 1971), p. 24.

[3] ibid., p. 26.

[4] 1 hectare = 2.47 acres.

[5] FAO: *Report of the Special Committee on Agrarian Reform,* op. cit., p. 28.

completely different patterns; but the background is still, in the main, one of subsistence or near-subsistence living for the small farmer and rural wage earner. In parts of the north thousands of peasants eke out a living, often as sharecroppers, on small plots of land under feudal systems of ownership. In the south old systems of communal rights to cultivate land still exist side by side with commercial exploitation. However, the former are either isolated from, or adversely affected by, the "money economy"; the result is that, despite the general relative sufficiency of land, the conditions of the majority of small cultivators fall steadily further and further behind those of the urban population. In the commercial agricultural sector, which consists mostly of plantations originally granted under colonial rule, the wage earners face problems of low wages and long hours; a lack of (or inadequate) housing, medical, sanitation and educational facilities; and inadequate safety provisions.

Furthermore, it has been estimated that by the end of the century, despite the expected migration to urban occupations, the rural areas of Africa alone will have to support 230 million more people than they did in 1970.

Questions and points for discussion

1. How many categories of rural worker can you identify in your local area? In your country?
2. What is the total working population in your country? How many work in agriculture? What is the percentage of rural workers in relation to the total working population?
3. How many of the rural workers in your country are sharecroppers or tenants? Small owner-occupiers? Agricultural wage earners? Nomads? Landless rural workers employed on a casual or seasonal basis?
4. Describe the main problems of life and work of the rural workers in your local area and in your country.

Rural workers' organisations

2

What are rural workers' organisations? .

There is a popular saying which runs: "In numbers there is strength." This saying is not quite accurate, however. Large numbers of workers of all kinds have remained in a state of poverty and ignorance for generations. It is only when workers organise themselves into disciplined and unified bodies that they acquire the strength and ability to overcome their difficulties.

A rural workers' organisation, like an urban or industrial workers' organisation, is formed by the coming together of a number of workers in an association established on a continuing and democratic basis, dependent on its own resources and independent of patronage, the purpose of which is to further and defend the interests of the members. A rural workers' organisation is a trade union or trade-union-type organisation of, for and by rural workers.

Let us look at the key words in this explanation.

Continuing. This distinguishes an "organisation" from a popular "movement", which is generally short lived and has no clearly defined structural form or financial basis.[1]

Democratic. The organisation must be operated "by" the rural workers to further and defend "their" interests.

Dependent on its own resources. Unless it receives fixed, regularly paid contributions ("dues") from the membership, the organisation will not have sufficient resources to further and defend the interests of its members; it will not have the power to decide whether it should be a "continuing" organisation if the resources come from another organisation or source, because the latter organisation will be able to make that decision; it will not be "of, for and by rural workers", as the contributing organisation can influence or determine its decisions.

Independent of patronage. As opposed, for example, to a union established openly or secretly by an employer to control the actions or demands of the workers.

---

[1] Note, however, that the word "movement" sometimes appears in the name or literature of bona fide rural workers' organisations as defined above.

Further and defend the interests of the members. This is the purpose of any association; if the association is one of workers, it is a trade union or trade-union-type organisation.

Rural workers' organisations are established and develop against widely different economic, social, cultural and agricultural backgrounds. For this reason they assume a variety of forms. These will be discussed in some detail in later chapters.

Why do rural workers' organisations exist?

Because of the varying economic, social, cultural and agricultural circumstances in which the world's rural workers live, their interests differ widely. Here it is possible to give only a brief idea of the variety of reasons why rural workers form their organisations. Three quotations have been selected to serve as illustrations. The first is taken from a report prepared by an Asian rural workers' organisation of sharecroppers, tenants, subsistence owner-occupiers and landless day labourers.

In developing Asia economic growth is straining at the leash of an iniquitous and outmoded social system. The extension of trade unionism to the countryside is necessary in order to apply much needed pressure for economic and social reforms and their effective implementation, to democratise the process of economic development, and to ensure the willing participation and involvement of the people, so crucial for its success. Nothing less than a thoroughgoing social and cultural transformation of the rural scene and the restructuring of rural society will meet the needs of the situation. The obvious need of the hour in almost all spheres of economic activity is thus organisation—organisation of planning to make possible the marriage of peoples' needs with available resources; organisation of work to make possible the full utilisation of labour; organisation of education to usher in institutional change; and above all, organisation of the masses to secure their participation in the economic effort and to ensure the equitable distribution of the fruits of growth.

The second quotation is taken from a speech made by a leader of a nationally and internationally known rural workers' organisation in a Latin American country.

The characteristics of land ownership, the conditions of life and the institutional systems of agrarian exploitation in the rural sector of underdeveloped countries have driven the peasant masses to develop two simultaneous and complementary courses of action. One is the organisation of peasants into unions. The other is agrarian reform. The basic objectives of these courses of action are the breakdown of the *latifundia* structure of land ownership and the creation of new kinds of labour relations that are different from those existing at present.

These objectives are also intended to improve the social, economic, cultural and political conditions of those living in rural areas, who generally constitute the overwhelming majority of the population. In order to convert the rural masses into market producers and active consumers, they must participate in social change within society —but within a society where they have hitherto been outsiders.

The political and economic structure of the underdeveloped countries has been determined by the predominance of land oligarchies. This domination is reflected in the legal institutions that facilitate the political submission of the people. For this reason the struggle for agrarian reform cannot be divorced from the political struggle but must create new links between social and economic forces so as to bring about the changes or revolutions that the new concepts of justice demand.

In the search for these new links, the existence of a rural workers' organisation is essential. The organisation must be concerned with the specific area of class, with a well defined programme and policy in which the individual is motivated to fight for his demands and which give practical and theoretical coherency to the movement. Simultaneously, the peasant must join political parties so that he can influence their policies and programmes from the inside and is able to get peasants' objectives, as planned in their own class-based organisations, included in the various parties' programmes.

The third quotation is taken from the constitution of a rural wage earners' organisation in a developed country. The written objectives of this union include the following:

— to unite under its banner all individuals employed as agricultural labourers, regardless of race, creed, sex or nationality;
— to negotiate, bargain collectively, contract or otherwise deal with the employers of agricultural labourers concerning wages, hours, working conditions, grievances, labour disputes and all other related matters;
— to secure recognition by employers and the public of agricultural labourers' right to organise for their mutual benefit and to engage in collective bargaining;
— to promote the development and maintenance of health, welfare and on-the-job safety practices and such educational training programmes amongst its members as would best effect a full knowledge of their rights, responsibilities, welfare and interest;
— to work and co-operate with other unions for the mutual benefit of the respective memberships;
— to strive for effective programmes which would improve, advance and increase the opportunity for employment;
— to promote a better understanding by government and the public of the purposes and objects of the union and the labour movement as a whole;
— to engage in legislative activity to promote, protect and advance the physical, economic and social welfare of the workers;
— to promote registration, voting, political education and other citizenship activities, involving the membership and their families and communities, which will secure the election of candidates and the passage of improved legislation;
— to engage in legal activities appropriate for the defence and advancement of the interests of the union and its membership;
— to distribute information to the members concerning economic, social, political and other matters which affect their well-being;
— to promote the full and equal participation by women in all affairs, activities and leadership positions of the union.

These three examples have been deliberately chosen from areas in which the situation of the rural workers themselves is widely different, in order to give some idea of the breadth of the answer to the question "Why do rural workers' organisations exist?" At the same time the range of economic, social, political and practical aims and objectives mentioned in these examples reveals that the variety is in fact infinite. In subsequent chapters we shall be able to look more closely at some of the ways in which rural workers' organisations seek to further the interests of their members—the basic purpose for which the organisations were formed.

Questions and points for discussion

1. Is there one (or more) rural workers' organisation in your local area? In your country? If so, what are the interests of the members that the organisation is furthering and defending?
2. Which of the members' interests has this organisation been successful in furthering and defending? Why? Which interests has it been less successful or unsuccessful in furthering and defending? Why?
3. If there is at present no rural workers' organisation in your local area, what interests would you want to see included in the programme of any organisation that you would help to organise and join?

Historical sketch of rural workers' organisations

3

Rural workers—whether slaves, serfs, tenants, subsistence owner-occupiers or wage earners—have rioted, rebelled, formed movements and gone on strike wherever and whenever economic, social and political exploitation by others have driven them to it. Throughout recorded history rural workers have been made aware of their mutual interests as a class or group. While our interest here is in "organisations", a review of some of the pre-organisation developments will be useful in helping us to understand the present situation.

The eighteenth and nineteenth centuries [1]

In Germany in the latter half of the eighteenth century most of the land was owned by the nobility, and the peasant was subject to a varying and complex set of legal systems. At one end of the scale medium-sized peasant holdings were subject to the property rights of the seigneurs, who leased them to occupiers on tenancies (usually of 6, 9 or 12 years), the "rent" being paid either in money or in kind or sometimes by a share of from one-quarter to one-third of the harvest. Remarkably, the tenant was compensated for any building he may have erected and for any improvement made; but he was required to grow certain crops, his tenancy had to go to his eldest son and he could be evicted if he failed to work the land adequately.

In the middle of the scale were those peasants who were born serfs or who became serfs by acquiring land subject to serfdom. They had certain obligations to the seigneur; without his permission they could not sell or mortgage the land, marry or take legal action, and they had to pay a fee to leave the domain. They were not "bound to the soil" as were serfs in the Middle Ages—with permission they could sell or exchange their tenure, and it was possible for a serf belonging to one seigneur to till the tenure of another.

---

[1] This section is based on information presented in Flores, op. cit.

But, at the lowest end of the scale, in certain regions of eastern Europe (Holstein, Pomerania, Mecklemburg, Livonia, eastern Austria and Poland) the seigneur held the power of life or death over the serfs and could if he wished sell them as slaves.

In Russia, where the peasants had been free during the Middle Ages, they came under bondage in the sixteenth century. From 1649 onwards they were in perpetual bondage as serfs and became part of the goods sold by the seigneur with the domain. In the eighteenth century they could even be separated from the land and be sold or exchanged as a simple piece of personal property.

On the other hand, in the south of Europe serfdom was unknown, but the peasants laboured under heavy taxes, were short of land and were ill paid. In some parts of Italy the peasant either farmed a small plot of land on the mountain slopes or was a tenant or sharecropper on the lands of the nobles in the plains. In other parts there were only day labourers working on the large estates.

In Portugal and Spain the same sort of situation existed. The peasants were free but destitute and laboured under social and economic structures which had changed but little since the sixteenth century.

In the mid-1840s a series of crop failures hit Europe. Potatoes failed in Ireland in 1845 and hundreds of thousands of people died; in Flanders, the Netherlands and Germany the potato crops failed a year later. Moreover, the bad cereal harvest of 1846 doubled or even trebled the price of wheat in western and central Europe. Since potatoes and cereals were the basic foods of the workers, the effects were far reaching. In England there was widespread unemployment and the workers organised strikes and looted shops. In France peasants and workers hampered and looted the grain convoys. In Belgium a revolt broke out early in 1847 which subsequently spread to the north of France.

This crisis in agriculture may be said to have triggered off in various European countries the series of revolts known collectively as the revolution of 1848. Although this rebellion against absolutism did not secure all the hoped-for reforms, for the peasantry in some countries it did mark the beginning of the end of the system of serfdom; and perhaps it may also be said that the peasants began to understand that only through collective action would they ever be able to improve their lot. As yet, however, there were no signs of the development of an "organisation"—the coming together of rural workers on a continuing basis. That story began in England—not among the peasants, but among wage earners.

The first rural workers' organisation

In England a much higher proportion of rural workers than elsewhere were wage earners. Farming in England had originally been based on a communal system, partly of open fields for cereal crops and partly of common pasture land. However, over the years the so-called "enclosure" system developed. This involved the fencing off of tracts of land to be farmed for the benefit of the landowners. The effect was that many of the peasants were left either without any land at all or with insufficient land to farm, and they became dependent for a living on working for a wage for those who farmed the enclosed land.

Between 1720 and 1840 some 6.25 million acres were enclosed. The enclosure movement may be said to have laid the foundations of modern British agriculture and to have contributed to the "release" of rural workers for employment in the fast-growing urban industries; but it also undoubtedly created a large and depressed body of agricultural wage earners whose conditions of life and work were little better than those of serfs.

The formation of workers' organisations was legalised in England in 1825 with the passing of what was known as the Combination Act. The very first such organisations were set up by urban workers in London and in the industrial north-west of the country; but the actual concept of organisation also spread to the countryside.

In the county of Hampshire, in the early part of 1831, the farm labourers gathered together (they did not form an authentic organisation) and succeeded in having their wages raised by approximately one-third, from 7s.8d. a week to 10s. The same thing happened in the neighbouring county of Dorset, and in the village of Tolpuddle the workers held several meetings with the farmers and landlords to discuss better conditions. With the local parson as witness, they eventually reached an agreement that their wages too should be raised to 10s. a week.

The employers never kept the agreement, paying only 9s. a week and subsequently reducing this to 8s. The farm workers, believing that the local magistrates had the power to fix wages, took their case to the local court. There the parson denied any knowledge of the original agreement, and the magistrates—all local landowners or clergymen—not only dismissed the case as being beyond their jurisdiction but also pronounced, in effect, that the men must work for any wage which the farmers might decide upon. The employers promptly reduced wages to 7s. a week and threatened to reduce them to 6s.

The workers' leader, George Loveless, had heard of the workers' trade societies (as the first unions were called) in the towns, and he sought the advice of two industrial trade union leaders. With their help the Tolpuddle Lodge (branch) of the Friendly Society of Agricultural Labourers was formed in 1833. This was the first known trade union for farm workers—the first known rural workers' organisation.

The news of the formation of the union quickly spread, and before it had time to take any formal action on behalf of its members the authorities reacted. Although the union was entirely within the law, the local employers, landlords and clergy, the judiciary and eventually the Government itself conspired to bring six of the members of the union to trial on what was afterwards established to have been a completely illegal charge. Early in 1834 a hand-picked jury ensured the men's conviction and the judge sentenced them to seven years' transportation to Australia as common criminals.

During the trial George Loveless handed the judge a piece of paper on which he had written their defence:

My Lord, if we have violated any law, it was not done intentionally; we have injured no man's reputation, character, person or property; we were uniting together to preserve ourselves, our wives and children from utter degradation and starvation. We challenge any man, or number of men, to prove that we have acted, or intended to act, different from the above statement.

But the men were transported in the prison ships and set to work in the convict settlements; and it was not until some time later that a few enlightened Members of Parliament and the industrial trade unionists were able to mount an effective campaign for the redressal of the injustice which had been perpetrated. Eventually the authorities were forced by public opinion to relent, and in 1836 all six men were granted a free pardon. After some delay all were brought back to their native land. Five of them were later assisted to emigrate to Canada; the sixth lived the rest of his days in Tolpuddle, and died in the workhouse there in 1891.

Subsequent developments

The ruthlessness with which the "Tolpuddle martyrs", as they have become known in trade union history, were treated was sufficient to discourage any similar attempt at organising farm workers in England for many years to come. It was not until 1872 that, from small local beginnings, a National Agricultural Labourers' Union was formed. This was immediately involved in both bitter strikes and lock-outs; but it did secure improvements in wages, and among other achievements it was instrumental in securing the vote for farm workers. However, lack of central control of both finance and policy, coupled with internal and political dissension, led to its demise in the 1890s. A farm worker and local secretary of this union founded, in 1906, an agricultural union which exists in the United Kingdom to this day.

In the late nineteenth century rural workers (both wage earners and self-employed) were also organising in other parts of Europe. By the turn of the century rural workers in most of western Europe had acquired the right to organise, though in some countries more years were to elapse before they had the right to strike. It may be said that by the time of the First World War rural trade unionism (mostly for wage earners) was firmly established, and in the 1920s "international" groupings (almost exclusively European) of rural workers' unions were emerging.

Today the three international trade secretariats [1] for farm workers have a

---

[1] The term "international trade secretariat" is used to denote the international organisation to which trade unions covering membership in a single trade or occupation are affiliated. In agri-

Eviction from tied cottages—a potential danger for rural workers in the nineteenth (above) and in the twentieth centuries (below)

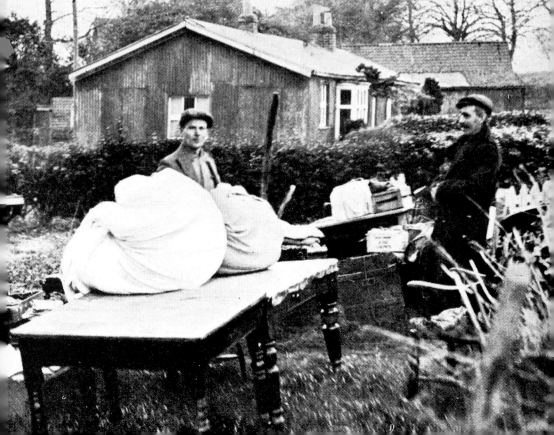

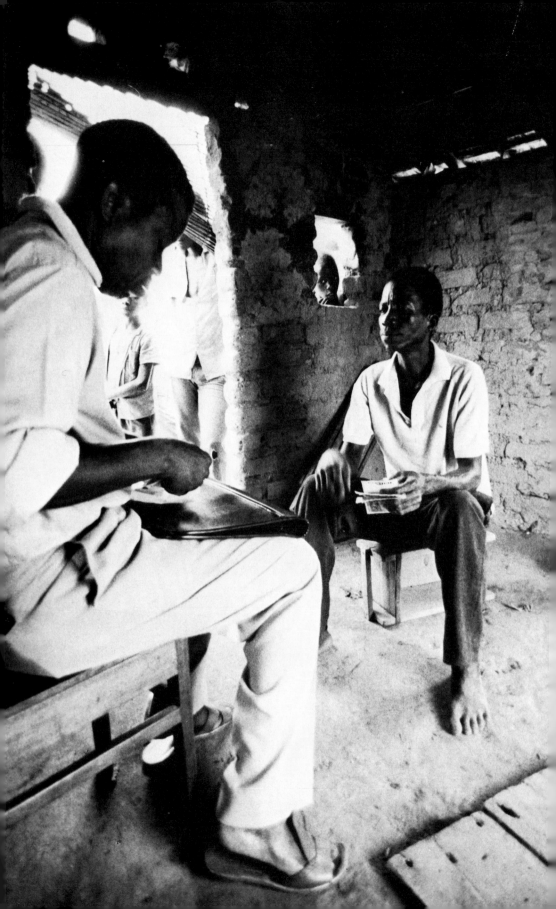

total of 40 affiliated European organisations in 29 countries. Whilst these are predominantly organisations of wage earners, they also include organisations of self-employed rural workers and some which cover both categories. The percentage of rural workers organised in Europe continues to increase, but at the same time the actual numbers of rural workers are declining as a result of the "drift from the land".

Rural workers' organisations outside Europe

In continents other than Europe the development of rural workers' organisations, like that of trade unionism in general, is a much more recent phenomenon. As in Europe (with perhaps one important exception), such development has usually been preceded by the development of trade unions in the urban and industrial sectors.

The exception is the plantation industry. It is often argued that trade unionism is a European idea, alien to the cultures of many non-European countries. Whilst there is clearly some truth in this, an additional and equally relevant factor as regards the rural sector is that, in much of the world outside Europe, the traditional rural system of agriculture (generally, but not everywhere, communal in character), together with the social, cultural and economic systems, was shattered wherever an equally European and alien concept—that of the plantation system of agricultural production—was introduced or imposed. The coming of the plantation system transformed local rural society, but subsequently the presence of large numbers of the new wage earners on the plantations made it easier to introduce the concept of trade unionism. In Asia, Latin America and Africa it was often in the plantation sector that rural workers' organisations first developed—sometimes in parallel with the development of urban unions.

In some respects the earlier struggles and gains of European trade unionists made the introduction of trade union concepts to other continents a little easier, but nevertheless progress was certainly not smooth. Even where the (mainly colonial) administrations were more or less sympathetic or neutral, the reaction of the employers and landowners was frequently one of repression. This, coupled with the extreme poverty and dependence of the workers, led to much hardship in the early stages; and this is still true in some countries even today.

The "Tolpuddle" stories of these countries have yet to be fully documented and recorded for posterity, but they undoubtedly exist—especially in the sector where the peasants have sought to organise in order to improve their lot vis-à-vis the big and often absentee landowners. When these stories

culture there are three main organisations of this kind: the International Federation of Plantation, Agricultural and Allied Workers (IFPAAW), the Trade Unions International of Agricultural, Forestry and Plantation Workers (TUIAFPW); and the World Federation of Agricultural Workers (WFAW).

are recorded they may well seem even worse than Tolpuddle by comparison, since most of the development of rural workers' organisations outside Europe occurred a century later than the events at Tolpuddle, and it would have been reasonable to assume that by that time attitudes towards workers and their rights might have been more progressive and liberal.

In *Africa* the development of rural workers' organisations seems to have lagged behind the major innovations in commercial agriculture. Although there is at least one case where an agricultural union was founded at the beginning of the present century, almost all existing rural workers' organisations date from after the Second World War. A few can trace their beginnings back to the early 1940s, many can do so to the 1950s; but there are also many which were founded only in the 1960s.

South of the Sahara most rural workers' organisations were founded as local or enterprise unions serving the wage earners on plantations. In most cases these gradually came together to form national plantation or agricultural unions. An interesting feature is that almost all the mergers led to the formation of a single national union, as opposed to a federation of autonomous units. On the other hand, in northern Africa the trend was towards the formation of federations (mostly for agricultural unions, as opposed to plantation unions). In one case the beginning of rural trade unionism was linked to the introduction of legislation on agrarian reform, which also provided for the right of rural workers to organise.

As different systems of trade unionism developed on the African continent, in some cases rural unions became a rural section within the national centre.[1]

The number of countries in which self-employed rural workers have the same right to organise as the wage earners is limited, and in some countries even the wage earners do not have the same right as the urban workers.

In fact, most of the organised rural workers in Africa are wage earners, but there are a few unions which also cater for the self-employed. At the present time, in Africa and the Middle East as a whole, there are known to be some 50 rural workers' organisations of all types in 38 countries; of these, 24 are affiliates of the three international trade secretariats for rural workers, and others have an associate relationship with these secretariats. But the percentage of organised rural workers remains very small and, when account is taken of the steady increase in the actual (as compared with the relative) numbers of the rural population, the percentage of those organised may well be on the decline.

In *Asia*, whilst in one country in particular there were peasants' or small farmers' movements in the period between the two world wars, the majority of rural workers' organisations developed during the era following the Second

---

[1] The term "national trade union centre" or "national centre" or "national confederation" is used to describe a national organisation which has as affiliates national workers' organisations of various occupations. In some countries there will be only one such centre; in others more than one, each having some political or sectoral affiliation.

World War. With a few notable exceptions, the trend has been towards the development of a multiplicity of small unions; these have frequently been very closely allied with, and often heavily dependent upon, political parties.

In the wage-earning sector the organisations are almost entirely confined to the plantations, though there are a few agricultural wage earners' unions. There are also a number of organisations which cater specifically for peasants and small farmers.

In a few cases the plantation unions have become, and have remained, dominant factors in the national trade union centre, and it is of interest that in these cases the organisations are of the centralised national union type. Elsewhere the trend has been towards loose and generally weak national federation structures—or towards no effective national grouping at all.

As in Africa, rural workers, and particularly the self-employed, do not always have the same right to organise as do urban workers, although (as is also the case in Africa) labour laws and trade union rights are fairly well established in the plantation sector, even if they are not always observed.

Again, the proportion of organised rural workers is low, and because of population increases in the rural areas is almost certainly declining. There are nevertheless well over 50 rural workers' organisations of consequence in 14 countries in Asia; some 37 of these are affiliates of the three international trade secretariats and a number of others have an associate relationship with them.

In *Latin America* the story is somewhat different, with some serious attempts to organise rural workers dating back to the early part of the present century. Moreover, a number of developments took place, both among wage earners and non-wage earners, during the 1920s and the 1930s. Almost certainly because of its agrarian structures and systems, Latin America is the continent where developments in the self-employed sector have equalled, if not outnumbered, those in the wage-earning sector. It is also a region where the trend is almost exclusively towards the federation type of structure, and in which those seeking to organise have encountered, and continue to encounter, reactions at least as harsh as those which faced the Tolpuddle martyrs.

Whilst there are organisations which further and defend the interests of both employed and self-employed rural workers, in most cases they cater either for peasants or for wage earners, the latter being concentrated in the plantation sector. There are examples of both types of organisation having won and maintained an influential place in the affairs of the national centre.

The history of trade unionism in the developing countries in general has always been influenced by the changes brought about by sharp shifts in the political character of governments. The traditionally volatile nature of politics in Latin America has led to constant changes in the fortunes of its trade union movements. The over-riding importance of agrarian reform issues in politics in this region has meant that the changes have often had more bearing on the developments of rural workers' organisations than on unions in the urban sector.

Both the *de jure* and the *de facto* right to organise in the non-wage-earning rural sector in particular are still a problem in many countries, and as in other regions the percentage of organised rural workers is, in general, certainly not high; however, the percentage of organised peasants is much higher in this region than in either Asia or Africa.

In the *Caribbean* the development of rural workers' organisations has been centred almost exclusively on the single agricultural economic base of most of the islands: the plantation sector. Although in a few cases agriculture is no longer the largest single income earner, it remains so for most of the countries in the area and the plantation industry remains a dominant factor.

Rural trade unionism, as established today, is largely a post-1945 development and is almost exclusively confined to the wage-earning sector. However, because of the small total working population on some of the islands, there has been a tendency to develop single general unions, in which the rural workers form a section within the general union structure. The extensive mechanisation and rationalisation of both the production and the processing sides of the plantation industries, coupled with the vicissitudes of world trade and large-scale commercial practices, have resulted in a sharp decline in the numbers of rural wage earners, so that they no longer have the dominant position they once enjoyed in the Caribbean trade union movement; nevertheless, despite the decline, the percentage of organised wage earners remains relatively high. Few, if any, of the rural workers who rely for their livelihood entirely on what they produce from their land are organised.

In Latin America and the Caribbean as a whole there are today almost 100 rural workers' organisations of consequence in 31 countries; nearly 70 of these are affiliates of the three international trade secretariats and many others have an associate relationship with them.

Questions and points for discussion

1. What do you know of the history of the economic, social and political life of rural workers in your area? In your country?
2. What is the history of urban and rural workers' organisations in your country? In your area? Has there ever been any event that might be called a local "Tolpuddle"?

Trade union rights and rural workers

4

Freedom of association for occupational purposes is, in fact,
but one aspect of freedom of association in general, which
must itself form part of the whole range of fundamental
liberties of man, all interdependent and complementary one
to another. [1]

The purpose of a rural workers' organisation is to further and defend the interests of its members. To form such an organisation, rural workers must be free to exercise the "right of association" and other rights which constitute the group of rights called "trade union rights". Urban, industrial and rural workers have had to struggle to obtain and defend these rights, and the struggle continues. Much has been written on the history of this struggle; here, in general terms, we shall examine the concept and status of the international labour standards relating to rural workers' trade union rights; the current status of national legislation concerning rural workers' trade union rights; and the ability of rural workers to exercise their trade union rights at the local level.

International level

The ILO and its role

The International Labour Organisation was created under the Treaty of Versailles in 1919, together with the League of Nations, and outlived that body to become, in 1946, the first specialised agency of the United Nations. Its original membership of 45 nations has now tripled in size. It is unique among world organisations in that workers' and employers' representatives have an equal voice with those of governments in the formulation of its policies.

The ILO engages in a wide range of activities in the labour and social fields, including:

— the formulation of international policies and programmes to help to improve working and living conditions, enhance employment opportunities and promote basic human rights;

---

[1] ILO: *Freedom of association and collective bargaining: General survey by the Committee of Experts on the Application of Conventions and Recommendations,* Report III (Part 4B), International Labour Conference, 58th Session, Geneva, 1973, p. 55.

— the creation of international labour standards to serve as guidelines for national authorities in putting these policies into action;

— an extensive programme of international technical co-operation to help governments to make these policies effective in practice; and

— training, education, research and publishing activities to help to advance all these efforts.

International labour standards

One of the ILO's oldest and most important functions is the preparation of international labour standards, which are then adopted by the tripartite (governments-employers-workers) International Labour Conference in the form of international labour Conventions and Recommendations. After a Convention has been ratified by a member State, that member State is under a binding obligation to put its provisions into effect. Recommendations provide guidance on policy, legislation and practice.

Between 1919 and 1977, 147 Conventions and 155 Recommendations were adopted. Together they have come to be known as the "International Labour Code". They cover many matters, including certain basic human rights (such as freedom of association, the abolition of forced labour, and the elimination of discrimination in employment), labour administration, industrial relations, employment policy, working conditions, social security, occupational safety and health, and employment at sea. More than 5,700 commitments to observe these Conventions have so far been made by member States.

Each member State is required to submit all Conventions and Recommendations adopted by the Conference to the competent national authorities for a decision as to the action to be taken on them. When a government has ratified a Convention, it must report to the ILO at regular intervals on measures which have been taken to implement its provisions. A country's observation of a ratified Convention is supervised by a committee of independent experts drawn from all parts of the world, and by a tripartite committee of the International Labour Conference. There is a special procedure for investigating complaints of infringements of trade union rights.

International labour standards and rural workers [1]

Because of the tripartite structure of the ILO, the interests of rural workers have been represented in the Organisation from the beginning. Indeed, the first Convention specifically dealing with the right of freedom of association of workers, adopted in 1921, covered agricultural workers.

---

[1] The relevant Articles and Paragraphs respectively of the ILO Conventions and Recommendation referred to in this section are reproduced in Appendix B.

Article 1 of this Convention—the Right of Association (Agriculture) Convention, 1921 (No. 11)—states:

Each Member of the International Labour Organisation which ratifies this Convention undertakes to secure to all those engaged in agriculture the same rights of association and combination as to industrial workers, and to repeal any statutory or other provisions restricting such rights in the case of those engaged in agriculture.

It should be noted that this Article covers the right of association of "all those engaged in agriculture" and thus applies not only to wage earners but also to the self-employed.

Over a quarter of a century later the Freedom of Association and Protection of the Right to Organise Convention, 1948 (No. 87), spelt out in detail a number of matters of concern to all workers (and employers). This Convention provides that all workers—without any form of distinction—shall have the right to establish and to join organisations of their own choosing; the only exceptions are members of the armed forces and the police. It also provides that such organisations shall have the right to establish and to join federations and confederations and also international workers' organisations. In addition, it contains provisions relating to the freedom of operation of workers' organisations and places on governments the responsibility for taking the necessary steps to ensure that workers can freely exercise their trade union rights.

This major instrument was followed a year later by the Right to Organise and Collective Bargaining Convention, 1949 (No. 98). This provides that workers shall be protected against anti-union discrimination in respect of their employment, protects workers' organisations from interference by employers' organisations (and vice versa) and promotes voluntary collective bargaining.

The comprehensive Plantations Convention, 1958 (No. 110), concerning the conditions of employment of plantation workers, was adopted in order to expedite the application to plantations of certain provisions of existing Conventions. It also contains provisions on freedom of association, the right to organise and collective bargaining, drawn from Conventions Nos. 87 and 98. Convention No. 110 was, however, confined to plantations situated in tropical and subtropical regions, and thus did not extend its protection to rural workers outside such regions. Nevertheless, this instrument was a major step forward. In addition to seeking to guarantee the trade union rights of plantation workers, it set out minimum standards concerning the engagement and recruitment of workers, wages, annual holidays with pay, weekly rest periods, maternity protection, workmen's compensation, labour inspection and housing and medical care.

But even though these Conventions had between them covered the rights of all rural workers, and specifically of plantation workers, it was still felt that there was a need for further standards to ensure the active encouragement and promotion of organisations of rural workers, including specifically those who are self-employed. For this reason the Rural Workers' Organisations

Convention, 1975 (No. 141), was adopted. One important feature of this Convention is that it clearly defines rural workers:

Article 2

1. For the purpose of this Convention, the term "rural workers" means any person engaged in agriculture, handicrafts or a related occupation in a rural area, whether as a wage earner or, subject to the provisions of paragraph 2 of this Article, as a self-employed person such as a tenant, sharecropper or small owner-occupier.

2. This Convention applies only to those tenants, sharecroppers or small owner-occupiers who derive their main income from agriculture, who work the land themselves, with the help only of their family or with the help of occasional outside labour and who do not—

(a) permanently employ workers; or

(b) employ a substantial number of seasonal workers; or

(c) have any land cultivated by sharecroppers or tenants.

The Convention then goes on to state that all categories of rural workers, whether wage earners or self-employed, shall have the right to establish and to join organisations of their own choosing; that the principles of freedom of association must be fully respected; that the organisations "shall be independent and voluntary in character and shall remain free from all interference, coercion or repression"; and that the law of the land shall not be such as to impair these guarantees. In addition it requires that it shall be an objective of national policy to facilitate the establishment and growth of voluntary independent rural workers' organisations.

The trade union rights of all categories of rural worker are thus firmly established in the International Labour Code. In addition, Convention No. 141 is supported by the Rural Workers' Organisations Recommendation, 1975 (No. 149), which spells out in detail the legislative, administrative and educational steps which need to be taken to ensure the effective implementation of the provisions and intent of the Convention.

National and local levels [1]

Rural workers and national labour legislation

The vast majority of countries recognise in law the right to organise of most, if not all, categories of wage earner. It is only in a few countries that trade union rights are not yet recognised for any type of worker or that the legislation is not applied in practice.

---

[1] This section draws heavily on a number of publications and documents: ILO: *Freedom of association and collective bargaining . . .,* op. cit.; Flores, op. cit.; ILO: *Le droit d'association des travailleurs agricoles dans les pays en voie de développement* (Geneva, 1974); and Gerrit Huizer: "Peasant organisations and their potential for change in Latin America", in *Land Reform, Land Settlement and Cooperatives* (Rome, FAO), 1971, No. 2.

However, there are some countries where freedom of association for agricultural workers is in effect not recognised in law, because these workers are excluded from the labour legislation which grants trade union rights to other workers.

Examples of specific limitations on the rights of agricultural workers which severely restrict their right to organise are more numerous. For instance, in some countries this right is not recognised on farms employing less than a certain number of permanent workers. This can mean that, in areas with a very high ratio of migratory seasonal workers to permanent workers (a ratio of 20 or more to one) and where there is a lack of communication, a total during the peak season of as many as 20,000 agricultural workers may not have been organised, despite appeals for help to this end.

The exclusion of agricultural workers from the national legislation which protects workers against acts of anti-union discrimination and promotes collective bargaining can also be, in practice, an obstacle to the development of occupational organisations within this sector or to their effectiveness in industrial relations. National legislation that prohibits industrial unions from undertaking any activities on behalf of agricultural workers can have the effect of depriving these workers of the assistance of the national trade union centre and has been known to make it impossible in practice for agricultural workers to organise.

A further example of the way in which freedom of association may be denied to rural workers is that offered by a country where, under the labour code, agricultural unions had to be "institutions of mutual collaboration between capital and labour", whose primary concern was "to work for the improvement of housing in rural districts". Organisations "whose methods of action are detrimental to discipline and order in employment" were deemed to be "contrary to the spirit and rules of the law".

Agricultural workers may also sometimes be denied their trade union rights through the prohibition or restriction of their right to strike. The ILO bodies charged with supervising the application of international labour standards have declared that the general prohibition of strikes considerably restricts the opportunities open to trade unions for furthering and defending the interests of their members and infringes the right of trade unions to organise their activities. Strikes in essential services, in which agriculture is sometimes included, are forbidden in a number of countries. The ILO has called attention to the abuses that might arise out of an excessively wide legal definition of the term "essential services" and has suggested that the prohibition of strikes should be confined to services which are essential in the strict sense of the term.

Examples may also be given of limitations on the trade union rights of all workers which particularly affect the rural sector, such as:

(a) long and complicated registration. In most countries that require the registration of a trade union the process is fairly simple, being little more than a formality. However, if the process of registration is long and complicated, it can lead to a restriction of the right of association, especially where the workers seeking registration are illiterate, ignorant of the law and its administration and living in an area that is remote from the capital;

(b) a requirement that all officers of the organisation should be literate. This can prevent the true representation of rural workers within their organisation, particularly at the local level; and

(c) the infringement of the right of workers' organisations to affiliate with international workers' organisations, through making such affiliation subject to government approval. This can deny educational assistance to rural workers' organisations that are in great need of it.

National legislation relating to the trade union rights of workers is often silent on these rights as they apply to self-employed rural workers—the share-croppers, tenants and small farmers. In some cases an examination of the labour legislation reveals that it applies to wage earners only, and therefore—unless (as is infrequently the case) the rights of association of the self-employed rural workers are covered by separate legislation—self-employed rural workers are precluded from organising on the same basis as their wage-earning colleagues. By clearly spelling out that self-employed rural workers are indeed "workers" and are entitled to the same trade union and civil rights as all other workers, the Rural Workers' Organisations Convention, 1975, may lead to the amendment of national legislation in some countries.

Practices and problems at the local level

Whilst the adoption of international and national laws relating to rural trade union rights is of course the essential first step, what is important to the rural worker is the application of those laws at the local level. Although in some countries matters of freedom of association, minimum wages and agrarian reform are all approached positively by governments and authorities at both the national and the local levels, this is by no means always the case; and even where the political intention is sound, the actual implementation is often less so. Thus, in practice, rural workers and their organisations may have to face a wide range of problems.

Since the large landowners in many developing countries may have an almost absolute control of economic, social and political life in the rural areas, there are many ways in which they can hinder the development of rural workers' organisations. One of the most common methods is to use economic and other sanctions against the initiators of the organisations. Agricultural wage earners who begin such activities may find themselves out of a job, unless they find ways to organise a group of colleagues in secrecy, or under the cover of a literacy club or mutual aid society. For the same reason tenants may be evicted from their land. Since there is often an unwritten agreement among the landowners in a certain area, rural workers who are dismissed or evicted by one landowner may find it very difficult to get a job or a plot of land elsewhere in the same region. Because the income of most agricultural workers and tenants is at the mere subsistence level, there is little chance that they will take the risk of losing their job or plot of land, since this could easily lead to starvation. The severe unemployment and indebtedness which exist in rural areas makes the risk of losing one's means of subsistence all the more serious.

These vestiges of feudal or semi-feudal organisation within some rural societies may prevent rural workers from exercising their trade union rights, even where national constitutions and national labour codes prohibit such archaic practices. The local agents of the law may or may not enforce or uphold the laws which recognise the civil and trade union rights of the rural workers to freedom of association, to organise, to collective bargaining and to strike action. These rights may be subordinated by the local authorities to the "property rights" of the landowner, either out of philosophical conviction or by virtue of some relationship with the large landowners.

In some parts of the world, the police have been, and in some cases still are, a serious impediment to the exercise of trade union rights and even a force in opposition to rural trade unionism. Some local or provincial police officers in rural areas remote from the national or provincial capital see trade unionism as a force of opposition to the authorities. Again, the police may be subordinate to local, provincial or even national authorities who may themselves be large landowners; or the police officials may have an economic, political or social relationship with large landowners.

A policy by the national government aimed at educating local police forces in the philosophy and purpose of trade unionism and in the rights of the rural workers and unions under the national labour laws and policies could do much to promote more tranquil industrial relations and to allow rural workers to exercise their trade union rights freely.

The experience of some rural workers with local prosecutors and judges in remote rural areas has been the same as with the police. The economic, political and social ties of the prosecutors and judges with the large landowners have made for an interpretation of the law that places the property rights of the landowners above the labour and civil rights of the rural workers. In areas where the large landowners are so powerful, it is difficult for the rural workers to secure someone to represent them legally in any case involving the local landowner.

In some parts of the world other methods and forces are used to deter the rural worker from forming or joining "an organisation of his own choosing". If the use of economic sanctions has failed to prevent the development of a rural workers' organisation, attempts may be made to buy off a leader by offering him money, land or access to a higher social status. If all other means have failed to undermine a growing movement, it has happened—and regrettably it still happens—that a leader has been assassinated.

27

These are the kinds of situation that lead rural workers to request outside assistance: from provincial or national rural workers' organisations if they exist, or from a national trade union centre. Urban and industrial workers' organisations will respond to such requests, because a denial of rights to one group of workers or citizens is in reality a denial to all—if not today, then tomorrow. All workers must stand together to protect their rights where they have already secured them, and to obtain them where they have not done so. Ultimately, only the workers, by "associating together to form an organisation", can "further and defend their interests"—including their right to freedom of association.

Questions and points for discussion

1. Read through the Conventions and Recommendations in Appendix B. How many of the Conventions have been ratified by your country?
2. What trade union rights are listed in the labour code of your country? Are agricultural workers mentioned? How? Are self-employed rural workers mentioned? How?
3. What is the situation in your locality regarding the ability of all rural workers to exercise their trade union rights? Do they need help? Where should they go if they need help?

Part II

Physical, constitutional, administrative and financial features

Physical features [1]   5

Earlier we defined a rural workers' organisation as the coming together of rural workers in an organisation which is on a continuing and democratic basis, is independent of patronage and depends upon its own resources; the purpose of this organisation is to further and defend the interests of its members. It is thus a trade union or trade-union-type organisation of, for and by rural workers.

Various types and forms of rural workers' organisation have evolved which reflect not only the category or categories of their membership but also the social, cultural, agricultural and trade union history of the country or area in which they exist. In this chapter we shall examine the physical features of rural organisations, and in Chapters 6 to 9 we shall look at their constitutional, administrative and financial features.

Types of organisation

Type by membership

An analysis of the physical features of rural workers' organisations by type of membership is useful in showing the variety of forms that exist; however, it must be understood that many, if not most, organisations are to some degree mixed organisations. Bearing this in mind, we may identify the following types of organisation.

1. Rural workers' organisations whose members are wage earners in agriculture. Such organisations are common in most countries of Western Europe, where their members are normally employed in small employing units. They are also found in many countries of Africa, the Americas, Asia and the

---

[1] This chapter, and also Chapters 6 and 7, are based on the working paper submitted to the ILO Symposium on Workers' Education Methods and Techniques for Rural Workers and Their Organisations, Geneva, 4-13 Feb. 1975 (doc. WED/S.30/D.1).

Caribbean, but in these countries their members are normally employed in several very large employing units (plantations).

2. Sharecroppers', tenants' and subsistence owner-occupiers' organisations whose members are self-employed agricultural workers. These exist in all continents but at present are more numerous in parts of Latin America.

3. Casual or migrant rural workers' organisations catering for workers in a farming area which relies on non-resident labour. Such organisations are rarely independent; where they exist, they are normally associated with general organisations of agricultural workers.

4. Organisations grouping two or more of the above categories of worker. Some examples of this type of mixed-membership rural organisation are found in all continents. However, organisations that bring together rural wage earners and self-employed rural workers are found in significant numbers only in Latin America and southern Europe, although their number is increasing elsewhere.

Type by structure

As regards structure too, there are variations and combinations. The following types of structure may be noted.

1. "Centralised" rural workers' organisations, which have a number of local units (branches, bases) and a centralised administration and policy. Such organisations include the national agricultural wage earners' unions in many countries of Africa, the Americas, Asia, the Caribbean and Europe; national unions organised on the basis of a single crop are also to be found—for example, the sugar industry workers' unions. The members of most of these "centralised" organisations include casual, seasonal and migrant workers as well as permanent workers. They often also include clerical and technical workers in agriculture, and some include all workers in the ministry of agriculture. In some organisations the members are self-employed rural workers. Most of these are at present in Latin America, but some "centralised" organisations in Africa, Asia and the Caribbean are endeavouring to organise rural self-employed workers.

2. "Enterprise" rural workers' organisations, which are formed to deal with a single employer. Examples are found wherever the plantation form of agriculture exists. However, there is a tendency for these organisations to merge to form one national organisation, with the original "enterprise" organisations becoming the local units of a "centralised" national organisation. Where they still exist, "enterprise" organisations have a centralised administration and most have permanent, seasonal and casual workers as members. They also generally cover all the types of worker on the plantation—agricultural, clerical, technical, and so on.

3. Federations of rural workers' organisations, which, as meant here, are composed of a number of autonomous local units affiliated loosely to the

co-ordinating federation. Examples are found in Africa, Asia and Latin America; but it should be emphasised that many rural workers' organisations whose name includes the word "federation" are, in reality, "centralised" organisations—the important distinction is that in one there is centralised administration and policy is determined at the federation level, whereas in the other there is merely a loose affiliation to a co-ordinating federation. The "federation" type of organisation generally stems from the coming together of many independent local rural workers' organisations. If the local units retain their autonomy, the new organisation is a "federation" in the sense in which the term is used here; if at its formation, or gradually at later stages, the policy, finances and administration are centralised, the federation becomes in reality a "centralised" organisation. Federations exist for all categories of rural worker and may have two or more categories of membership.

4. General workers' organisations, which are organisations catering for workers in all occupations, including rural occupations. Examples of general workers' organisations with rural workers as members are found in Europe and some of the smaller countries in Africa and the Caribbean. Economic and historical reasons underlie their formation: the number of wage earners in these countries in the urban occupations, in industry and in agriculture was not sufficient in economic terms (i.e. membership dues paid to the union) to make it possible to form strong, separate unions for each occupation. Consequently, one large union was formed of all workers, with sections at the headquarters level for the different groups of worker. These are "centralised" organisations and, as regards the rural sector outside Europe, their membership is generally made up of wage earners on plantations. However, there is growing interest among these unions in organising the sharecroppers, tenants and small owner-occupiers.

5. Rural workers' sections of a national trade union centre, which are trade or occupational sections (in this case for rural workers) within a national centre. There are great differences in the degree of autonomy of such sections. Examples are found in Africa, the Americas, Asia, the Caribbean and Western Europe, and again the general reasons for their existence are economic and historical. Outside Europe they were formed by the national centre when not enough rural workers had been organised to form an economically sound organisation capable of furthering and defending their interests. A percentage of the dues of workers in urban and industrial workers' organisations paid to the national centre is used to service those rural workers who are organised and to help to organise other rural workers until they are numerous enough to form a national rural workers' organisation. In some cases these rural workers' sections result from a general restructuring of the national trade union movement, involving the setting up of new national centres having a number of broad trade (occupational) sections.

In a few of the smaller countries in Europe the situation is different: here the *percentage* of rural workers organised in a national union is high and continues to increase, but the *number* of workers in agriculture is constantly decreasing as a result of mechanisation in agriculture and the need for more workers in industry and services. As a result, membership in the national union has been constantly decreasing, and in order to economise on administration, research, rent, salaries, and so on, these centralised national agricultural unions have become centralised autonomous sections within national federations or centres.

Questions and points for discussion

1. How would you classify the rural workers' organisation or organisations in your area and in your country as regards "type of membership"?
2. As regards "type of structure"?
3. How has the organisation evolved as regards type of structure?
4. In your opinion, is the evolution now complete or is further evolution necessary?

Constitutional features

6

The constitutions of rural workers' organisations are a reflection of the types of interest the organisation has been formed to further and defend; of local and national conditions and history; and of the stage of development of the organisation. It is difficult to cover in any depth the variety of constitutional forms that exist in rural workers' organisations around the world. Here we attempt to suggest the broad outlines of the major forms. To assist in assessing the relationships between the various constituent parts of the organisation, a possible diagrammatic structure is set out in figure 1. This represents a typical "centralised" structure and is intended only as an illustration—an illustration which can easily be adapted in order to suit local circumstances and needs.

Base or local unit

The base or local units within a rural workers' organisation are usually defined in the constitution and are referred to under a variety of terms, for example, the branch, base, section, subsection, local, union,[1] league (as in peasant league, community league, indigenous league), estate or plantation or local or ranch committee, and so on. The base unit is generally a village or community—or, in the case of some rural wage earners' organisations, an estate, plantation or *hacienda*, or a subdivision of these.

Whatever they are called, the base units all serve as the first point of contact between the member and his[2] organisation, and they are normally the

---

[1] The term "union" is often found among the base units of wage earners' organisations in some parts of Latin America and south-west Europe; the workers formed their union on a local basis in the first place, but on affiliating to a national organisation retained their original name.

[2] Or "her", for (as has already been observed) in some parts of the world there are large numbers of female wage-earning rural workers and in others women are self-employed, assisting their husbands or members of their family who are sharecroppers, tenants and subsistence owner-occupiers. It is important that this point be borne in mind whenever, for reasons of brevity, the word "his" is used in the text. Normally women have the same rights and responsibilities within rural workers' organisations as men, and sex is one of the aspects covered by the term "without discrimination" in Article 4 of Convention No. 141.

Figure 1.   Constitutional structure of a typical rural workers' organisation

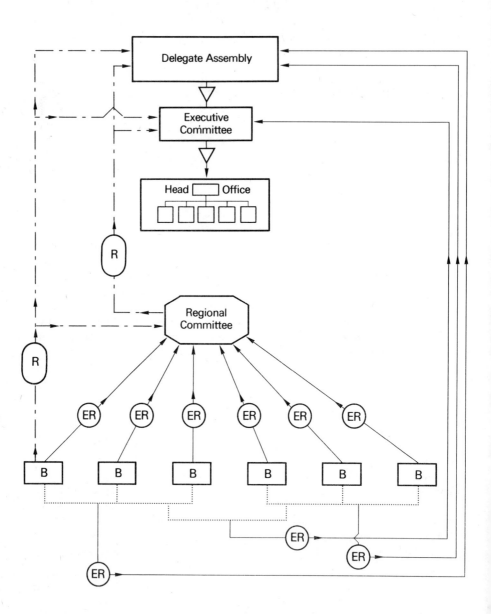

point where the member pays his contribution (dues). It is here that the member brings his problems to be solved and where he raises the interests he wants to be furthered and defended. It is also at the base unit that the member can seek to influence the policies of his organisation and, conversely, that the organisation's policy can be made known to him.

The effectiveness of any rural workers' organisation in furthering and defending the interests of its members depends on the effectiveness of the base units and ultimately upon the involvement and interest of the local members. But much also depends on the local leadership—the secretary, president or chairman of the base unit, who is normally an elected voluntary (unpaid) officer.[1] It is important to the base unit that the members give him as much assistance as possible to enable him to carry out his duties and responsibilities effectively.

Regional or occupational committees

In many large rural workers' organisations regional organisations have been set up between the base unit and the headquarters or federation. These regional committees vary in importance but have the common function of acting as spokesman and pressure group with the authorities and/or employers at the same level, of helping isolated base units or units with difficult problems, and of assisting in organising localities or rural workers that are not yet organised.

In some organisations with several categories of rural worker, and particularly federations and general workers' unions, there are occupational committees or sub-organisations between the base units and the headquarters or federation; these are based on the various categories of rural worker, and therefore we find committees or sub-organisations of wage earners, of sharecroppers and tenants, of subsistence farmers, of community or peasant or indigenous leagues, and so on.

The officers of these regional or occupational committees are normally voluntary elected workers, and here again the effectiveness of the committees is very much dependent upon the officers and the assistance and co-operation they receive from the base units. These committees or sub-organisations hold assemblies of delegates from the base units. The assemblies decide regional or occupational policy and elect regional or occupational officers.

Delegate assembly, conference, congress or convention

This meeting of elected delegates from the base units (and from the regional and/or occupational units) is often named in the constitution as "the

---

[1] The term "officer" is used throughout to denote voluntary workers elected to office; the term "official" is used to denote a paid member of the staff of the organisation (who may be either appointed or elected).

supreme authority" of the organisation. The constitution also often provides that, subject to that authority, the organisation shall be governed between delegate assemblies by an executive committee or council. The delegate assembly normally has the power to make or reshape or change the policies of the organisation and (although this usually requires a two-thirds or three-quarters rather than a simple majority) even the rules. It is also generally the body which elects the principal officers and officials. Under the constitution it meets at specified intervals (normally every two or three years); in situations of extreme emergency it can be called into extraordinary session by the executive committee. It is at this assembly of delegates that the coming together of rural workers to form an organisation "on a continuing and democratic basis" literally has expression. The elected representatives of all the members have the opportunity and obligation to review what the organisation has done, what it is now doing and what it should do in the future. The success of such an assembly and its effects on the future of the organisation and on the members is dependent, on the one hand, on the extent to which the members and delegates have been kept informed of developments between and during assemblies and are thus capable of exercising knowledgeable and responsible judgements; and, on the other, on the success or otherwise of the leadership of the organisation in keeping itself informed on organisational and national affairs and on the real problems, feelings and interests of the members. Only a knowledgeable membership choosing knowledgeable leaders and making responsible judgements can succeed in furthering and defending the interests of rural workers.

Leadership

The leadership of rural workers' organisations generally consists of the elected executive committee (this can be composed of voluntary officers or full-time paid officials, depending on the size and economic strength of the organisation) and the president and general secretary, who are also elected and are generally also members of the executive committee. In this latter respect there is a great variety of situations: some organisations have both a president and a general secretary, both of whom are full-time paid officials; some have only a president, and in some the president is a voluntary officer. Generally (but not always), where the president is a full-time paid official he is the principal official of the organisation; where the president is a voluntary officer the general secretary is the principal official.

In the larger rural workers' organisations there are other officers or officials with specific responsibilities such as organising, finance, education, agrarian reform, and so on. In some cases the members of the executive committee are assigned or elected to these specific "secretariat" functions.

In addition to the executive committee, some rural workers' organisations have a directory council which is ranked between the delegate assembly and the executive committee as regards both its powers and the frequency of its meetings. These appear to be historical and mainly regional in origin (being found especially in parts of Latin America). They generally meet every six months and often have some, but not all, of the powers of the delegate assembly. However, they would not, for example, have the power to change the constitution or to elect the national executive committee.

Questions and points for discussion

1. What is the "base unit" of the rural workers' organisation in your area? Why is it formed as it is?
2. What is the "supreme authority" under the constitution of your organisation? How often does it meet? How many delegates are there? How are they chosen?
3. If elected as a delegate to an assembly, how would you prepare yourself for this role?
4. Using figure 1 as a reference, prepare a diagram illustrating the constitutional framework of an organisation with which you are familiar, showing the elements of membership participation and control in the affairs of that organisation. If the framework differs from that illustrated in figure 1, what are the comparative advantages and disadvantages of the two frameworks?

Administrative features 7

In order to obtain the best possible results, every organisation must use its resources—i.e. the personnel and finance available—efficiently and effectively. This is particularly true of rural workers' organisations, which, in many parts of the world, have a huge potential membership (50 per cent or more of the working population) very much in need of an organisation to further and defend their interests; but the members and potential members are generally scattered about the countryside and have only a very limited income.

The administrations of rural workers' organisations vary widely according to the needs and stage of development of the organisation. There is, however, a common broad pattern in what they are trying to achieve, and it is particularly worth noting that the more durable and effective organisations of rural workers all have well developed central administrations, control systems and finances.

While some points of this chapter are made in earlier and later chapters also, the importance of good administration to the success of a rural workers' organisation makes that repetition worth while. A graphic presentation is again provided (see figure 2) of the administrative relationships between the various units of the organisation. It is intended only as a guide and is based on the same kind of structure as that used for figure 1; it can thus be easily adapted to suit other circumstances.

Objectives of administration

The main objectives of administration are normally as follows.

1. To ensure and maintain the financial basis. One of the main activities of administration in any organisation has to be the management of finance. This is all the more important for a rural workers' organisation, particularly in developing countries, because of the low incomes of their members and because of their general lack of experience in accounting procedures. It is essential that every means be adopted to ensure the regular collection of the

Figure 2. Administrative structure of a typical rural workers' organisation

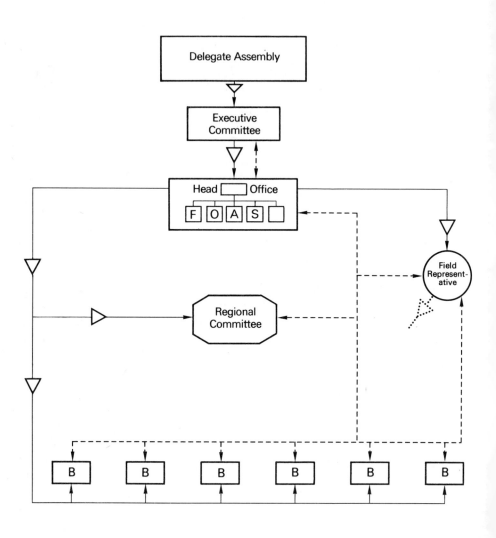

▽ = Decisions / Instructions   --▶ = Communications   B = Base or
                                                                Local Unit

F = Finance   A = Administration

O = Organisation   S = Services

contributions of all members, and that the dues collected be properly administered—both at the local and at the national levels. This means that the administrative procedures have to be developed and defined so that all involved at base, regional and central or national levels fully understand and can effectively carry out their individual and collective responsibilities in this field.

2. To maintain and extend the membership of the organisation. Without members the organisation can have neither influence nor finance; without influence and finance it cannot further and defend the interests of its members. Organising and retaining members, which may often be difficult in the rural sector, is crucial to the life and success of the organisation and must be a main objective of administration. Again, procedures have to be developed to ensure that all involved at branch, regional and headquarters levels understand and can play their individual and collective roles with regard to recruiting and retaining members.

3. To achieve effective communication. There must be an effective two-way flow of information and communication between the various levels and units of the organisation. In the rural sector this is complicated by the scattered nature of the membership and the modest financial and personnel resources likely to be available. But without some system, however simple, the organisation cannot function. At the very least (but by no means the least important) there has to be a means of regular verbal interchange of views and news between base, regional and national units.

4. To provide a service to members. This is the reason for which the organisation exists. Proper service cannot be given unless the preceding three factors have received proper attention; but at the same time the organisation will not be able to survive unless it does provide the maximum possible service to the membership—thus, to ensure that the organisation does in fact "further and defend the interests" of members is the one administrative objective to which all the other objectives have to be geared.

Elements of administration

The main physical considerations of administration can be said to be the following.

1. At the base level. In organisations of rural workers, the work at the local level is generally dependent on voluntary part-time officers who must also earn their living in agriculture. Administration has to be designed to take account of these limitations and also the fact that, because of the isolation in which they often have to work, those at the local level may have to carry a greater load than is the case in urban and industrial workers' organisations.

2. Field representatives. Any effective rural workers' organisation of any size will have one or more "field representatives" who visit each base organ-

isation regularly and, in addition, any unit faced with a problem or emergency. Depending on the country and the organisation, these field representatives are referred to as organisers or organiser/educators or activists or representatives or business agents. They are full-time paid officials and are usually appointed by the national or federation executive committee. Although there is seldom any provision for them in the constitution of a union, they play a crucial role in the successful development, operation and administration of a workers' organisation. They are expected to be specialists in many fields: organisers, educators, advocates, administrators, negotiators, conciliators. They represent and are at the service of, on the one hand, the local members and their base organisation and, on the other, the executive committee.

Where an organisation of rural workers is not yet sufficiently strong in numbers and financial resources to employ field representatives, it falls to the full-time officials on the executive committee to perform these functions when an emergency arises. It is not easy, however, for these officials to spare any of the time that they have to devote to their own important national duties. In any case, the union members at the base units need the services of field representatives not only in emergencies but regularly.

3. Every member a voluntary activist. At the local level the field representative and the local officers can do much to foster and improve the four main objectives of administration. So, too, can the local members. Some can offer to help the officer in charge of dues collection by covering certain areas. Most members will know some rural workers in the area who have not yet joined the local organisation and, under the guidance of the local officer responsible for organisation, they can assist in this work. Others can help to pass on to isolated areas the information received from the national level and to obtain information on the situation and conditions in these areas for transmission to the base organisation and then to the national level. Depending on the service or the project, many members can be voluntary assistants to the local officer responsible for these.

In this way, administration at the local level will be greatly improved and the field representatives and other national officials will be freed to devote their time and efforts to improving administration at the national level.

4. At the national level. The general secretary or president, depending on who is the principal official, is constitutionally responsible for administration within the organisation. At the national level he can guide the executive committee in appointing or nominating the members most qualified for the various "secretariat" functions (organising, finance, services, education, and so on). He can observe the status of administration within these functions and provide remedies or education where problems exist. Similarly, he can observe and assist in solving administrative problems at the regional and local levels. It is his responsibility to see that the tasks of financial accounting, collecting dues, maintaining communications, organising and servicing are carried out in a timely and efficient manner.

Advantage should be taken at every opportunity of any educational programmes and seminars initiated by the national workers' movement, in order to improve the administrative knowledge and capabilities of all officials and officers at all levels.

All officials and officers below the level of general secretary or president are responsible for improving the administration of their own functions and for assisting and guiding those responsible for the same functions at lower levels.

Ultimately, the responsibility for correcting ineffective administration, where it exists, falls upon the members, who, through meetings of base units and through sending properly instructed delegates to the regional committees and the delegate assembly, can exert pressure for improvements and can, if such a step proves to be necessary, elect a new official or officials more competent in matters of administration.

Questions and points for discussion

1. What are some of the reasons that might make administration more difficult in a rural workers' organisation than in a factory workers' organisation? Easier?
2. If you were appointed to a committee to evaluate the administration of your rural workers' organisation, what questions to be answered might you put on your list?
3. Do you have any ideas how you personally might be a "voluntary activist" in a base organisation?
4. Using figure 2 as a reference, prepare a diagram showing the administrative units and indicating the flows of decisions and communications in an organisation with which you are familiar. If it differs from the system in figure 2, what are the comparative advantages and disadvantages of the two systems?

Financial features: 1

8

There are three usual sources of income for workers' organisations: members' contributions or dues; money that has been invested; and external sources. Income from dues is always the most important (whether or not it is the largest) source of finance, for it is a measure of the members' willingness to support their organisation—a barometer indicating whether they feel the organisation is providing them with the services they require. Income from investments is, of course, dependent upon whether an organisation's total income is greater than its over-all expenditure. Income from external sources is generally dependent upon an organisation's demonstrated or potential ability to manage its affairs successfully.

We shall now look at some important aspects of both contribution income and income from external sources. It will perhaps be helpful to use an analogy to introduce the subject. If we consider that the physical features we have discussed are the "flesh" of the organisation, that the constitutional features are its "bones", and that the administrative features are its "nerves and muscles", then we might think of the financial features as the "life's blood" of the organisation.

Need for finances

A postage stamp and an envelope to advise the national headquarters of a problem with a local landlord, employer or government official; a telegram to announce the expulsion of some sharecroppers or tenants from the land they were tilling, of a flood in the locality, of a local strike; a legal document to be prepared for a case involving the rights of an indigenous community; research into the cost of living of the workers and the profits of the local plantation, necessary for collective negotiations for a new contract; technical assistance for a small project in community development—all these items in the furtherance and defence of the local interests of the members require money, at either the local or the headquarters level, or both.

Moreover, to further and defend the interests of the rural workers at the national level requires even more money, in order to pay for the full-time paid officials and staff who are needed, first, to respond rapidly and effectively to requests for assistance from the local level; second, to represent the interests of rural workers in agrarian reform legislation, and in agrarian institutes, banks and marketing boards; third, to represent rural workers in negotiations over labour legislation dealing with minimum wages, hours, working conditions and health and safety standards; and fourth, to represent the families of rural workers in the struggle to obtain social security and educational and health care facilities in rural areas.

A local rural workers' organisation which is not a part of a national organisation can itself accomplish very little for its members, even at the local level. It can accomplish nothing at the national level. Even such an isolated organisation needs some money. If it is really to be in a position to further and defend the interests of rural workers, an organisation must be organised from the local level up to the national level—the only level where many of the problems of the rural workers can be solved.

Nature of members' contributions

How much money is needed? Or, to expand the question a little, how much money is needed by rural workers' organisations to be strong enough to further and defend the interests of their members? Not as much of this type of information is available as might be wished, but there is enough to reach some general conclusions.

Let us take first the case of organisations of rural wage earners. There is, for example, a very large and strong union in the plantation sector in Asia which applies a single rate of dues for all members, regardless of their wages; thus, while the lowest-paid workers pay 1.66 per cent of their wages in dues, the higher-paid workers pay a lower percentage. Many European organisations of rural wage earners also charge a fixed rate of dues to all members, regardless of what the members earn. In one, the members earning the average wage pay 2 per cent of their wages in dues; those earning less pay a higher percentage; those earning more pay a lower percentage. In a strong African union, there are three rates of dues; one rate for those earning below NU 50[1] per month, a higher rate for those earning between NU 50 and NU 70 per month and the highest rate for those earning above NU 70 per month. Even here, the lowest-paid members pay, on the average, 1.25 per cent of their wages in dues, as against an average of 0.5 per cent paid by the highest-paid members. One North American union of rural wage earners operates a fixed percentage system, under which all members pay the same percentage of their wages. The amount paid thus varies according to the wages received.

---

[1] NU = national units of currency; see the explanation given in the preface, p. vi.

Rural workers' meetings may be held in the open air (above) or in a member's home (below)

Turning next to organisations of self-employed rural workers (share-croppers, tenants, subsistence farmers), we find that there is even less information. The data that are available indicate that the percentage payable in dues is generally a little lower than in rural wage earners' organisations, but is in most cases a fixed amount for all members. Hence those with the lowest income pay the highest proportion of their income in dues. The figures available range from 0.5 to 2 per cent.

The limited data available nevertheless allow us to make two important observations: *(a)* there is a general tendency for those members with higher incomes to pay higher amounts of money in dues to their organisation, but those members earning lower incomes pay a higher percentage of their income in dues; *(b)* all rural workers' organisations that are providing a worthwhile service to the members apply dues rates that vary from 1 to 2 per cent of members' incomes; most rates stand at 2 per cent of the income of the lowest-paid members.

How much money is needed, therefore? Experience and the available statistics indicate that at least 2 per cent of the income of the lowest-paid members is needed to build a strong and effective rural workers' organisation.

Ability to pay

Are rural workers, with their low incomes, able to pay enough in dues to build an effective organisation to further and defend their interests? The answer is that rural workers *have* done so, and that more are doing so every year.

Those who think rural workers cannot pay enough often make the mistake of converting the average income of rural workers in developing countries into the "strong" international currencies (dollars, francs, sterling, etc.); by taking 2 per cent of the converted figure they arrive at a ridiculously low amount of annual dues for each individual member, in terms of dollars, francs or sterling. But of course, the overwhelming majority of the rural poor do not live in areas where these moneys are earned, or spent.

Let us try a new approach. Let us go to a developing country, which we may call X-land, where the minimum wage by law for day labour in agriculture, performed by rural workers who are also sharecroppers, tenants and subsistence farmers, is NU 5 per day. Because there are not enough government labour inspectors in the rural area to enforce the law, the rural workers in this region actually receive only NU 3 per day. The income from their work as day labourers, plus the value of their share of their annual production as sharecroppers and tenants, adds up to an average income for this poorest group of rural workers of NU 900 per year. If 2 per cent of the income of the poorest member of a rural organisation is deducted as dues, we arrive at a membership due of $(900 \times 2 \text{ per cent} =)$ NU 18 per year from the poorest group.

These trainee field representatives will play a crucial role in the activities of their organisation

But in this one region of X-land there are over 200,000 rural workers in this category. Even if only 50 per cent are organised, the *minimum* annual income to their organisation is $(100,000 \times 18 =)$ NU 1.8 million.

So far we have considered only the workers with the lowest incomes. If the dues are 2 per cent for all, regardless of income, the annual amount received by the organisation from these same 100,000 workers could well be doubled, to reach NU 3.6 million.

In addition, there are 50,000 permanent agricultural workers on the plantations in the next area of the country, half of whom are also members of the same organisation; 2 per cent of their incomes (which average more than four times those of the first group) adds another NU 3.6 million to the income of the organisation, giving a total of NU 7.2 million. And there are two more agricultural regions in X-land!

Is a sum of over NU 7 million enough to finance an effective national rural workers' organisation?

It is in X-land, because it will pay for office rents and the salaries of officials at the national level, even though these may well be higher than those in the areas where the members live;[1] and it will pay for field representatives working at the local level, and for the many other things necessary to make an organisation effective.

This illustration is based on the situation in a real country, and there are many countries like it; but it can be argued that our example is not applicable to those countries (for example, in some parts of Asia) where the vast majority of rural workers are landless labourers. They have no land, nor access to land, in order to supplement their income, which is dependent upon what they can earn from such day work as they can find—and over the year the number of days on which they can find work is very low. However, in almost every case the number of workers for every square kilometre is much higher than in X-land—it can even be ten times as great. In terms of income for an organisation, therefore, although 2 per cent of the individual incomes of these very poor workers is extremely small in itself, the potential number of members from whom it can be collected can be counted in millions. Thus the annual income of the organisation can still amount to millions of NUs; and, within that country, those millions have sufficient value to pay for and to provide, both at the national and at the local level, the staff and services necessary to further and defend the interests of the members.

Methods of collection of dues

While the sum represented by 2 per cent of the income of the poorest workers in the rural sector, when multiplied by their huge numbers, is enough

---

[1] In the country on which these calculations were based an official in the capital city would be paid around NU 5,000.

to maintain an effective rural workers' organisation, there are other problems.

How do you collect NU 7 million?

In the second region in X-land (sugar plantations) the methods of dues collection adopted have been applied to agricultural wage earners in all parts of the world. The 25,000 plantation workers mentioned above are employed on 200 sugar plantations, with from 50 to 500 workers on each. There are two methods of collecting the members' dues. The first and oldest method is through "collectors"—fellow workers who are generally voluntary officers—who go to see the members assigned to them on pay-days and the days immediately following. They collect the 2 per cent dues from their fellow members and give each member a receipt. At the same time, the collectors exchange information with the members. This is two-way communication within the organisation—an important aspect of the good administration we discussed earlier.

The second method is the "check-off system",[1] which is sometimes found on very large plantations or where one company has many workers in one area. With this method the members sign a form authorising the employer to deduct 2 per cent of their pay each pay-day and to send it to the union. This system has the advantage that it is economical for the rural workers' organisation, in that the voluntary officers can then spend their time on other organisational activities; but it does have the disadvantage that the regular opportunity for two-way communication between officers and members is lost.

Thus, through collectors and the check-off system, one-half of the NU 7 million can be collected. But what of the first region of X-land, with 100,000 members scattered over hundreds of square kilometres of valleys and mountains? There could easily be hundreds of base organisations to be visited; but the most difficult problem is that there is no regular pay-day every month. When they work as day labourers the rural workers in this region are paid at different times, and except at harvest time they have no cash income at other times of the year.

The collection of dues on a regular monthly basis is not feasible in such regions. New methods of collection must be found. The ability to pay is there—the problem is how to collect the dues regularly. The only solution that has been found so far is to carry out the collection once a year.

This obviously simplifies matters for the collectors, but what about the members themselves? Is it easier for a member in this region to pay NU 1.5 each month or NU 18 once a year? Clearly, having regard to their circumstances, it will generally be easier for this category of member to pay in cash once a year—provided that the payment is always made at the same time each year and that the annual payment is related to the economic, cultural and

---

[1] For a more detailed description of the check-off system see E. Córdova: "The check-off system: A comparative study", in *International Labour Review* (Geneva, ILO), May 1969.

social life of the community.[1] Obviously, in this region, payment has to be made some time after the harvest, when the sharecroppers, tenants and subsistence farmers have had an opportunity to sell some of their share of their production. It should be emphasised that the concept which links the annual payment of dues for self-employed rural workers to some aspect of local rural life is one that must be adapted to circumstances in each country and, in some countries, in each region.

Two simple examples illustrate possible methods of implementing such a scheme. First, some countries maintain the practice and tradition of an "identity card" which is used in civic and business life. Although the majority of rural workers in these countries do not have such cards, they know and accept their purpose and importance. This system can be copied by introducing an "organisation identity card", issued and renewed annually, following the harvest. This card would identify the rural worker as a member in good standing with his organisation and as one entitled to participate in all its activities, meetings and decisions and to benefit from all the services provided by it. The member in the first region of X-land would pay NU 18 for his organisation identity card and another NU 18 each year for its renewal.[2]

Another method (which, ideally, still involves the use of the organisation identity card) is illustrated by our second example. This is to tie the collection of the annual dues to some event, fête, saint's day or public holiday which is part of the local culture. Some rural wage earners even have a paid holiday to celebrate the date of the foundation of their union, and this idea might well be extended. On such occasions of public celebration the amount which even very poor people spend is many times more than 2 per cent of their annual income, and if the tradition of paying the annual union dues at the same time could be established many potential difficulties could be overcome. Nevertheless, such a system must be approached with caution. In many cultures the rural people frequently borrow money for the celebrations (generally from money-lenders at exorbitant rates of interest); it would be wrong for the organisation to institute a system of collecting union dues which tended to put members even further into debt—even if for only 2 per cent of their annual income.

The collection of dues on an annual basis among the poorest of the rural workers is possible; it does, however, call for adaptation to the circumstances of each culture and country.

---

[1] In the country we have called X-land, NU 18 buys three or four bottles of local beer or six glasses of the local alcohol in a public drinking place in the communities where these members live. The cost of a live chicken at the weekly farmers' market in the region is NU 36—i.e. two years' dues.

[2] One of the advantages of this system is that it reduces figure work to a minimum. No receipt need be given to the member, provided that a new card is issued each year; the collector has only to record the names of the members and to produce cash for the number of cards with which he was supplied minus the number he has not "sold".

Distribution of dues

After they have been collected at the local level, where do the rural worker's dues go—to his local organisation, or to his national organisation? As we saw earlier, the strongest rural workers' organisations tend to be "centralised" in their administration.[1] Under this system all funds are sent to the national level and a percentage is returned to the local level and to the regional level. In practice the proportions vary considerably, but in general not less than 90 per cent remains at the national level, with 10 per cent or less going to the regional and/or local levels. Several points should be made here. A very large percentage of the money retained at the national level is actually used to maintain field representatives who spend almost all their time working with and assisting the local organisations; another significant percentage of the money at headquarters level is spent on direct assistance to individual members or local organisations in trouble, particularly on legal assistance. On the other hand, the staff in the regional and local offices are, or ought to be, all part-time and voluntary officers, and the local "office" of the organisation is often the home of the current local president or secretary. Thus only a small amount of money is needed for paper and postage. If there is a small local emergency, members can and do "pass the hat round".

In the case of federations (i.e. autonomous base organisations loosely affiliated to a national organisation), members' dues are distributed in the proportion of 5 to 25 per cent to the national federation and the remainder to all levels below. As 5 per cent of NU 3.6 million is only NU 180,000, there is insufficient money to maintain field representatives, to provide emergency help to a base organisation, or to employ technical personnel at the national level in order to further and defend interests at that level.

The present trend in rural workers' organisations seems to be towards the formation of mixed organisations (i.e. composed of both rural wage earners and self-employed rural workers), which are "federations" in the sense that each category is represented individually within the national organisation but is "centralised" as regards administration and finance, with 90 per cent or more of the dues going to the national level.

External sources of finance

Some rural workers' organisations, for a variety of reasons and in a variety of circumstances, have accepted and received financial assistance from sources outside the organisation—that is, from sources other than the dues of their members or investments.

---

[1] Figure 3 shows typical flows of finances in such an organisation. As in the case of figures 1 and 2, it is intended only as an illustration, which may be adapted to meet local circumstances.

Figure 3. *Financial structure of a typical rural workers' organisation*

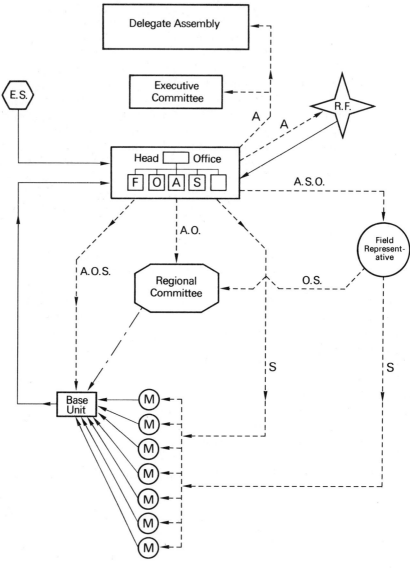

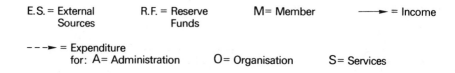

E.S. = External   R.F. = Reserve   M= Member   ——▶ = Income
      Sources   Funds

---▶ = Expenditure
    for: A= Administration   O= Organisation   S= Services

Early development

When a rural workers' organisation is just getting started, finances can be a serious problem. Where a national organisation is being formed by the merger of financially strong local or regional organisations, there is little or no difficulty. However, if the organisation is being formed by only a few local organisations which are financially weak, some outside assistance may be necessary. Traditionally, this assistance has come from other workers' organisations. Two representatives of an urban workers' organisation went to Tolpuddle at the request of the local rural workers to assist in forming the first known rural workers' organisation. Later, in various difficult periods (particularly strikes), urban and industrial unions and the national centre gave financial assistance to the English rural workers' organisations. This story has been repeated throughout the world. As just one example of many, a world-wide workers' centre [1] is assisting financially in the formation of an organisation of landless rural workers in an Asian country where no such organisation exists at the moment.

Project money

Even when they are fully developed, rural workers' organisations may need financial assistance for initiating certain types of special service [2] for members. This type of assistance can take the form of a gift or a loan or a combination of both. These projects might be in housing, medical services, co-operative-type production, marketing or consumer activities, and so on. The financial assistance is limited to the specific project or service, and the assistance is given either in a lump sum or over a specified limited period. The most important point is that the organisation is not dependent upon this type of assistance for its normal activities, nor for its survival as an organisation. Generally, such assistance comes from or through other workers' organisations, such as an international trade secretariat of rural workers; or it may come from international or national governmental or non-governmental organisations interested in rural development.

Political parties

Both at the time of their formation and as a regular practice, some rural workers' organisations have received financial assistance from a political party within their country. In these situations the relationship of the rural workers' organisation to the political party varies from one where the organisation is an integral part of the party (in such a case the agrarian secretary of the party

---

[1] The term "world-wide workers' centre" is used here to denote an international workers' organisation to which are affiliated national trade union centres. There are three main organisations of this kind: the International Confederation of Free Trade Unions (ICFTU); the World Confederation of Labour (WCL); and the World Federation of Trade Unions (WFTU).

[2] The question of special services for members is dealt with in more detail in Chapters 12 and 14.

might also be the president of the organisation) to one where the party contributes a large sum of money to the organisation each year.

Government subsidies

In some countries legislation provides that the government may financially assist workers' organisations for specific activities, which are generally educational in nature. In a few countries the parliament has voted to pay a sum of money each year to subsidise a rural workers' organisation. This is not the same as "project money": the money goes towards the educational or general expenses of the organisation, in the latter case on a continuing basis.

There are thus two main uses of external financing: for specific projects to initiate special services for members; and for the general expenses necessary for the operation and survival of the organisation. It will also be noticed that the external sources are themselves of two main types: other workers' organisations, and organisations which are not workers' organisations.

The situation of a rural workers' organisation which is dependent on assistance from outside to further and defend the interests of its members can best be illustrated by two sayings: "He who pays the piper calls the tune", and "What governments (or political parties) give, governments (or political parties) can take away." It cannot be over-emphasised that, however well intentioned donors may be, their influence is always present. In particular it is important to remember that governments change and political parties disappear—a matter which was the subject of a resolution adopted by the International Labour Conference in 1952, which stated that: "When trade unions in accordance with national law and practice of their respective countries and at the decision of their members decide to establish relations with a political party or to undertake constitutional political action as a means towards the advancement of their economic and social objectives, such political relations or actions should not be of such a nature as to compromise the continuance of the trade union movement or its social or economic functions irrespective of political changes in the country."

In other words, while an organisation that is "continuing", that is "independent of patronage and dependent on its own resources", and that is run "for and by rural workers" may be able to achieve more in a shorter space of time by the use of external sources of income, it must ultimately be able to depend for its survival on the dues of its members alone.

Questions and points for discussion

1. What is the average annual income of the lowest-paid group of rural workers in your locality?

2. Would 2 per cent of the above figure multiplied by half the number of rural workers in your country be a sizable amount? Would this sum pay for the salaries and

working costs of an effective union office in the capital city, and for field representatives?

3. Would the collection of dues be a problem in some parts of your country? How would you adapt the idea of an annual collection of dues to the rural culture of your country?

4. What do you think is the right division of income between national and local levels? Is this the distribution adopted in organisations which you know?

5. Using figure 3 as a reference, prepare a diagram of the flows of finances of an organisation which you know. If it is different from the system in figure 3, what are the comparative advantages and disadvantages of the two systems?

Financial features: 2   9

It is important that all members of an organisation should have a clear understanding of the general financial procedures of that organisation, and this is our purpose in this chapter.[1]

Once an organisation has achieved a sound financial footing, based on a dues system of 2 per cent or more of the income of its members, what does it do with the money? First, the organisation must receive it and account for it—it must record how much money is received, and from whom; and how much is paid out, to whom and for what. Second, the organisation must have regulations to control the use of the members' money. Third, the leaders of the organisation must make the best possible use of the money in furthering and defending the members' interests; they must therefore make a plan or budget as to how much will be spent on different activities and items. Fourth, the officials must make periodic financial reports to the members explaining how much money was received and how it was spent.

The proper administration of the organisation's finances is vital to the success of the organisation. Like all organisations, a rural workers' organisation, in order to be effective and strong, must use its income wisely. An organisation is not necessarily strong just because it has a large amount of money; it can be strong only if its leaders administer its finances well.

It must always be remembered that a union obtains its income from its members. The members *are* the union, and the money belongs to them. If the officials are careless in their administration of the finances, the members will become disenchanted and the organisation will become weak. If the officials can demonstrate to members that they are using the money in the members' best interests, there will be solidarity among the members and the organisation will be strong.

Apart from the system of collecting, how can members be persuaded to pay their dues readily? The surest way is to keep the members informed about

---

[1] For those who are in any way directly concerned with the management of finances, more detailed guidelines are needed than are set out here. See Appendix A, pp. 121-130.

how, and on what items, their money is being spent. This involves both education and communication. During any meetings of the organisation the officers should give a report of the financial position. They should outline what services are being rendered to the members and what activities the organisation is undertaking, and explain the cost involved. If the officials introduce effective programmes which meet the needs of the members, they will pay their dues more readily.

When workers' organisations receive money from their members, it is important for them to set up a proper system of accounts. This system will vary according to the needs of the particular organisation. However, basically all accounting systems try to achieve the same objective: to record the income received, and to record the money paid out. When a simple system of accounting has been set up, the treasurer can easily prepare a report of income and expenditure which will help the officials and officers to run the organisation more efficiently. A report of this nature should be released to the members every three months to inform them how and for what purpose their money is being used.

The dues collector

Except in the case of unions which have negotiated a check-off agreement with the employer, a rural workers' organisation must collect the dues from the members through a "collector", either on a monthly basis from its wage-earning members or on an annual basis from its self-employed members. If this process is to work smoothly, the collectors must recognise the importance of their position. They not only collect dues but also serve as a link between the organisation and its members, informing the members of the organisation's meetings and activities; and they are often the first union official to hear a member's problems. A good collector will also encourage non-members to join the organisation. The collector must be an energetic, responsible and loyal member.

A rural workers' organisation should have sufficient collectors to contact each wage-earning member at the same time each month or to contact all self-employed members within a few days where annual dues are paid.

Dues received from members should be recorded immediately in ink in a "collector's book" (see example, figure 4) and the members must be given a receipt or new annual membership card, or have the amount they pay recorded on their existing membership card.

The total amount of dues received by the collector should be handed over within a specified period (in some unions it is 24 hours) to the person responsible for cash in the unit concerned (the treasurer[1]). The treasurer will then

---

[1] In some organisations the office of treasurer does not exist at the local level. However, whatever the title may be, all constitutions will provide for the election of a person with responsibility for finances at the local, regional and national levels.

Figure 4. Specimen page from a collector's book

Date	No.	Name	Amount	Total	Arrears	Remarks	Received by (Treasurer's signature)

Figure 5. Specimen cash receipt

No. _____	Date _____
Received from _____	
the sum of _____	
_____	
for _____	
_____	
Amount _____	Signature _____

sign the collector's book and issue a form of receipt (see example, figure 5) to the collector for the money received.

Membership records

At the organisation's headquarters a membership register must be kept. The headquarters treasurer records the dues payments in the membership register (see example, figure 6) from the collector's book.[1] In the case of monthly dues, such a record will show whether the member is "paid-up" or in arrears. Every three months a list should be compiled of the members in arrears and given to the collectors concerned so that they may investigate the reasons for the arrears. In the case of those members paying annually, the membership register will be adapted accordingly.

Basic financial regulations

The following basic financial regulations will serve most rural workers' organisations as a means of controlling the handling and use of money at the local, regional and national levels:

— the organisation should keep a cash book for receipts and payments;

— payment vouchers should be used for all moneys paid out and official receipts given for all moneys received; they should be pre-numbered and bear the name of the organisation;

— all entries in any of the accounts books should be written in ink;

— no erasures should be made in any records and accounts books; incorrect entries should be corrected by bold cancellation of the wrong figure and the insertion of the correct figure above it or next to it, with the writer's initials;

— all records and accounts books should be kept under lock and key when not in use;

— in the event of a cancellation of a receipt, the word "Cancelled" should be written between two diagonal lines over the original, with a carbon impression on the copy; the copy should be left in the pad;

— receipt books should be issued by the principal official (general secretary or president) only to the treasurer, who should sign for them;

---

[1] All the examples reproduced in the figures in this chapter and in Appendix A are based on actual forms which were produced for workers' education purposes by a national trade union centre and which are being used by its rural workers' affiliates.

Figure 6. Specimen page from a membership register

No.	Name	Address	Joined	Arrears (brought forward)	Jan.	Feb.	Mar.	Apr.	May	June	July	Aug.	Sep.	Oct.	Nov.	Dec.	Total	Arrears	Remarks

— the accounting system should follow a double-entry book-keeping system;[1]

— all moneys received, whether in the form of cash or cheque, should be deposited in the organisation's bank account within 48 hours;

— the maximum amount of cash which the treasurer is allowed to hold should be stipulated (depending on the size of the organisation);

— no payment should be made unless it is authorised by the rules of the organisation;

— the treasurer should be provided with an adequate cash box;

— all cheques drawn must be properly filled out before being signed by the treasurer and at least one, and if possible two, other members of the organisation;[2]

— a statement of income and expenditure should be submitted to the general membership of the organisation at least once a year, and if possible twice a year;

— the treasurer must be ready to produce all books and records to the trustees[3] when required.

These rules may seem both commonplace and elementary, and so they are; but they have been set out in detail because organisations, both rural and urban, have run into difficulties over money matters at local, regional or national levels for want of observance of one or more of them. If the rules are followed faithfully, and provided that the members exercise their rights and duties to scrutinise and question accounts at the local, regional and national levels, the possibility of something "going wrong"—a possibility in any human institution, large or small, of workers or of academics—is reduced to a minimum.

In order that these rules may be followed it is necessary to establish certain minimal book-keeping, accounting and auditing procedures. The purpose and outcome of such procedures are vital to *all* members of a rural workers' organisation: unless they understand how their membership dues are looked after and how they have been or will be spent, they cannot effectively exercise their rights and responsibilities to influence and control the financial affairs of the organisation—affairs which ultimately control the extent to which it furthers and defends their interests.

However, the detailed application of such procedures is of crucial importance only to those officers and officials who, at local, regional or headquarters levels, are (or may be) responsible for receiving, keeping and spending the organisation's money. For those people, and for those who

---

[1] A method of book-keeping in which every transaction is recorded in two places—in one place as a debit to one account, and in a second place as a credit to another account.

[2] This provision is normally set out in the constitution of an organisation and usually specifies the persons concerned, e.g. the president and/or the general secretary.

[3] See p. 126.

would assist them, the details—the "standard" procedures which are not peculiar to rural or even to workers' organisations—are covered more fully in Appendix A.

Questions and points for discussion

Very few people will be elected as treasurer of a rural workers' organisation at the local, regional or national level. But it is essential for the health and democracy of the organisation that members should be able to understand the financial statements of their organisation. Even those members who are unable to read can ask another member to explain it to them.

1. Review the year-end financial statement of your rural workers' organisation. Do you understand all the items and entries?

2. Assume that you are responsible for the administration of the moneys in that financial statement. Which items of expenditure do you think should be increased? Decreased? Added? Eliminated? Why? Is the level of income from members' contributions as high as it should be, having regard to the number of members? If not, why has this happened?

3. Assume that you are the principal officer of your local rural workers' organisation. Your local budget (remembering that the greater part of the members' dues goes to the national level) is NU 200. What proposals do you think you should make to the members concerning the use of this money for various items and activities? Did you save some for "emergencies"?

Part III

Servicing the interests of rural workers

So far we have briefly examined the various categories of rural worker; considered their conditions of life and work; defined a rural workers' organisation; outlined part of the history of those organisations; looked at the trade union rights of rural workers at the international and national levels and the practice of trade union rights at the local level; and examined some of the physical, constitutional, administrative and financial features of rural workers' organisations.

Here we look into the reasons for which a rural workers' organisation exists. What are the interests of rural workers that are furthered and defended by their organisations, and how do those organisations set about their task?

Since providing services for the members is the only reason for the existence of a rural workers' organisation, we shall look in some detail at the kinds of interest with which such organisations are concerned and the general methods used to provide the services in question. In Chapters 10, 11 and 12 we shall consider some of the main types of service provided for rural wage earners by their organisations; in Chapters 13 and 14 we shall consider services for self-employed rural workers.

Bargaining activities for rural wage earners 10

Among the foremost interests which rural wage earners expect their organisations to further and defend on their behalf are, naturally and traditionally, their wages and conditions of employment. There are two principal methods for regulating wages and conditions of employment: by legislation on minimum wages, or by a collective agreement reached as a result of negotiations between a trade union and an employer or an association of employers.

The existence of minimum wage fixing machinery is often a sign that the circumstances of the industry and the degree of organisation of the workers are such that the latter are not in a position to use legitimate industrial pressure either to achieve their demands or to enforce any agreement that might be reached. The enforcement of the agreed minimum rates is a matter of law, and defaulting employers may be prosecuted in the courts by the government's wages inspectors.

In contrast, the existence of a collective agreement is normally an indication that the workers are sufficiently well organised to bring effective pressure to bear in order to secure the agreement, and the enforcement of the terms reached is generally dependent upon the initiative of the union and perhaps ultimately on the unions' industrial strength.

The two systems of regulating wages may often be found side by side. Where minimum wage fixing machinery exists, a union may, if it is strong enough, negotiate a collective agreement with an employer or a number of employers for terms and conditions better than those provided for by law.

Minimum wage fixing machinery varies from country to country. In some the legislation may provide for a minimum wage for ali workers, regardless of their occupation or industry; in others there may be separate minimum wages for specific industries, and all industries or occupations may not necessarily be covered by the legislation. In some cases the minimum wage is determined by government decree; in others it is determined by a wages board or council. These latter bodies are normally tripartite in character, being composed of representatives of workers and employers and government nominees; the decisions of these bodies must generally be ratified by the government before they become legally effective.

In those cases where a minimum wage for rural workers is determined by government decree, the task of the rural wage earners' organisation is to make representations to the appropriate department so as to secure the best possible conditions. In the case of a wages board or council, the organisation's task is one of direct bargaining on these bodies. However, these representational or bargaining functions often have their limitations, and where unions feel this to be the case they tend to rely heavily on pressure-group activities.[1]

The range of the items that may be covered by minimum wage fixing machinery varies considerably. The legislation may provide only for the fixing of a minimum hourly rate of pay. In some cases it may provide for a weekly rate, for the number of hours in the working week, for overtime and for holidays with pay. In a few cases it also extends to such matters as shift rates, "plus" rates (skill differentials) and wages during sickness. But as a general rule the terms and conditions of employment covered under minimum wage legislation are far fewer than those which may be covered under collective agreements.

A collective agreement is a written document, signed by both the union and the employers, which specifies what has been agreed during the bargaining between the two parties over wages, hours and conditions of work.[2] Depending on the interests of the workers and the strength of the union, the agreement may cover many other items. Some collective agreements covering agricultural workers are as short as two pages, others are as long as 100 pages or more. The proposals or demands that the members wish to be put to the employer(s) for negotiation are generally formulated by the executive committee or by a special "bargaining committee" of the union, and are based on information received from the members of the local units of the national union. Here again, two-way communication is vital to the success and strength of a rural workers' organisation.

The following pages provide a summary review of workers' interests as illustrated by examples drawn from collective agreements that have been negotiated with employers by rural wage earners' organisations in different parts of the world (mainly in the plantation sector). It will be seen that the range of members' interests that are furthered and defended in collective agreements is very wide, and that there is a variety of methods for attaining these aims.

Wages

Wage clauses and their detailed appendices are generally the longest sections of collective agreements. The wage schedules may apply to piece-

---

[1] See Chapter 11.

[2] For a comprehensive treatment of the processes and practices of collective bargaining see ILO: *Collective bargaining: A workers' education manual,* 10th impr. (Geneva, 1976).

rate, hourly, daily and monthly paid workers. In the appendices to the agreements, the job classifications can vary from, in one case, a total of six for the hourly, daily and monthly paid workers plus four piece-rate items to, in another case, 315 for the hourly, daily and monthly paid workers plus 295 piece-rate items. The more complex job classification schedules in the hourly, daily and monthly paid section are generally agreements in the sugar sector which include the workers in the sugar factories.

Most agreements contain provisions for overtime and "plus" rates.

The wages provisions in many agreements provide for various increments of an annual nature, which are dealt with below.

Cost-of-living increases

These are provisions under which wages are tied to increases in the cost of living, either by using annual figures published by the government or, more commonly, by annual renegotiations on this matter only.

Bonus systems

There is a considerable variety of bonus clauses. There are "production bonus" clauses which provide for an annual cash bonus to all workers, based on the production on each plantation during the year in relation to pre-set production targets. There are "incentive bonus" arrangements providing for cash bonuses to the workers on an individual basis, for individual production over an agreed norm—for example, pounds of latex brought in by a rubber tapper. There are also a few "price bonus" arrangements under which there is an automatic percentage increase in the earnings of all workers if there is an increase in the price received by the employers for the agricultural commodity (such as sugar, rubber, etc.). Some arrangements provide for an "attendance bonus"—although it is usually called by another name—under which workers receive a cash bonus based on the number of days actually worked during harvest time. Occasionally there are clauses covering an "annual bonus", with the actual amount being left to the employers to determine.

Pay record provisions

This serious problem and interest of the workers is dealt with in a number of agreements. Under one of the strongest clauses on this subject the employer is required to keep full and accurate records, including total hours worked, piece-rate or incentive records, total wages and total deductions; and to give to each worker every pay-day a copy of the itemised deductions as well as his piece-rate production record. This clause also provides that for any specific grievance on this subject the union shall have the right to examine time sheets, work production or other records relating to a worker's earnings.

Work or pay guarantee arrangements

Some agreements provide for the payment of wages or their equivalent for piece-rate work when, for various reasons, no work is available. The more common arrangements of this type apply to bad weather conditions which make field work impossible, and provide that such days shall be treated as days worked with full pay and benefits. Another type of work guarantee provides, for example, that if the employer is unable for any reason to offer work to a worker for an extended period, the worker will be guaranteed a minimum of 20 days' pay in each month.

The availability of "reasonable work" is of special interest to piece-rate workers, and some agreements have special clauses to service this interest of members. One agreement covering workers on tea plantations provides that if there is insufficient leaf to provide full employment for all pluckers, those workers who are surplus to requirements shall perform other work at a stated daily flat rate (which corresponds to average piece-work rates). An agreement covering workers on banana plantations provides for a higher rate of pay for spraying a "hard acre" than for spraying an "ordinary acre", both being defined in the agreement. The same principle is also found in agreements relating to work in rubber plantations, where fields of rubber trees are classified as "low yielding" and "high yielding" and carry different piece-work rates.

Equal pay for equal work

A few collective agreements in the rural sector have clauses covering this principle. One example states that the employer shall recognise the principle of equal pay for equal work irrespective of sex; another states that the pay and workload of women workers shall be the same as for men in the same grade.

Paid leave

Paid public holidays

Most collective agreements provide for paid public holidays. The usual provision when work is performed on such holidays is that the workers shall be paid at twice the normal rate. Provision is made in the agreements for considering piece-rate workers as being employed on a daily basis as regards their entitlement to paid holidays. To this end some agreements stipulate that the legal minimum wage shall apply, while others provide for a specific higher rate.

Paid annual leave

Collective agreements for rural wage earners also generally provide for paid annual leave; the requirements for eligibility vary greatly, however, as do

Rubber tapping, a typical piece-work job

the amounts of leave earned. One case provides that the workers, after working 200 days in any calendar year, shall receive five paid days for one year of service; ten days for two to eight years of service; and 15 days for over eight years of service. Another provides one-and-a-half days of paid leave for each month worked. A third provides that all workers with more than one year of service shall receive 20 consecutive days of annual leave with pay; this agreement also provides that temporary workers who work during the whole of a harvest shall receive 11 days of paid leave.

Paid sick leave

Many agreements contain provisions for paid sick leave, and these also vary greatly. One example provides that workers are entitled to 21 days of sick leave in any one year. Another lays down that workers with not less than three months of service are entitled to paid sick leave of up to 14 days in each year if they do not have to go to hospital, and up to 60 days if they do; this agreement also provides that, in cases of tuberculosis, cancer or leprosy, workers are entitled to sick leave for every day spent in a hospital, up to a maximum of nine months at any one time. The rate of sick pay in such cases is full pay for the first 60 days and half pay for the remaining part of the nine months.

Redundancy and retirement provisions

Redundancy and severance pay

Clauses dealing with redundancy appear in most collective agreements, many providing that the principle of "last in, first out" shall apply. Some agreements are silent on the period of notice to be given to workers before they are laid off; those that contain negotiated minimum periods of notice stipulate one week to one month.[1] Not all agreements make provision for severance pay, but those that do so have requirements for eligibility varying from one to two years of service. On severance pay itself the middle of the range is about two weeks of pay for each year of service for the first three years, and three weeks for each year over three years.

Retirement benefits

Although in some countries all or part of the workers may be covered under a national social security scheme, only a few collective agreements contain retirement benefit arrangements. One major agreement provides for the retirement for all agricultural workers—permanent, temporary and seasonal—on a national basis. The employer and the worker each pay into a pension fund 5 per cent of the amount of wages paid to the worker. Under

---

[1] It is possible that those agreements that do not specify the length of notice to be given do not do so because the national labour laws already set a minimum.

Rural workers' organisations are greatly concerned
by the dangers inherent in the use of toxic
chemicals in agriculture

73

another major agreement a pension fund has been set up which is managed by a committee of three representatives of the rural wage earners' organisation and three representatives of the employers. Under this agreement the contributions into the fund are made entirely by the employers: a flat amount is paid for each kilogram of sugar produced, with the amount per kilo being increased if the price of sugar goes up.

Death benefits

Whilst this item is not found very often in collective agreements for rural workers, a few do contain certain provisions: for example, a flat amount (say, about three months' wages) may be paid to the family of the deceased worker.

Health and safety provisions

Agreements negotiated by rural workers' organisations do not generally contain clauses concerning health and safety,[1] but those that do have such clauses show a growing concern with chemicals. One example provides for the establishment of a joint worker-management committee for the prevention of accidents, with a government agency providing advice and with the on-the-job knowledge of the workers and supervisors being used to improve safety standards. Another agreement requires that workers who fumigate fruit crops and control weeds with chemical products must work to a three-month rotating cycle and that any worker who is allergic to the chemicals shall be transferred to other work.

One agreement has a lengthy section on this matter, stating that the company "agrees to consult with the union's health and safety committee in formulation of policy" in this field. This consultation includes all matters related to the health and safety of workers but specifically covers the use of toxic substances; the use of certain highly toxic pesticides is expressly prohibited. Moreover, the company agrees to notify the union committee about the application of poisons and, in consultation with the union committee, to determine the length of time during which workers are to keep out of a treated field; the company also agrees to keep weekly records, which will be made available to the union, concerning:

— the location of the field treated or to be treated, if practicable;
— the pesticide or poison used, including the brand name, the registration number on the label, and the manufacturer's batch or lot number as shown on the label;

---

[1] In a few countries minimum standards on safety and health in employment in agriculture, especially in relation to the use of chemicals, have been established by law. In such cases the organisation may seek, through representation, to bring about improvements in such standards; it may also seek to have higher standards included in the collective agreement.

— the dates and time of each application, if practicable;

— the amount of each application;

— the formulation and concentration in spray or dust;

— the method of application;

— the name(s) of the person(s) applying the pesticide or poison; and

— the estimated date of the harvest.

This agreement also requires that, when organophosphates are used, "one baseline cholinesterase test and other necessary cholinesterase tests" shall be taken on those workers applying the pesticide or poison, and that the organisation and the worker shall be given the test results immediately.

Employer-provided housing

The need for housing for wage-earning rural workers and the problems connected with this need are reflected in many collective agreements. Where there is not enough housing in the plantation sector, some agreements provide for a flat-rate monthly housing allowance. More common, particularly in one region, are clauses requiring the employer to build a specific amount of new housing of specified size and materials in each year of the agreement; to repair existing housing; to demolish a specified amount of compound-type housing each year; and in some cases, to set up a joint committee to assign housing on the basis of years of service and size of family. Many agreements require the installation of electricity, water and sanitary facilities.

Medical facilities and services

In many developing countries there are very serious shortages of medical personnel and facilities; social security does not cover medical services, and private services are very expensive. In the plantation sector in particular, the need of members for medical services is often the subject of collective bargaining. Even in those countries where by law plantations of a certain size are required to provide medical services, the matter is also often covered by collective agreements because the standard required is often very low.

The many items covered include, for instance, the size of the medical facility which must be maintained; the professional qualifications of doctors, nurses and pharmacists required to staff the services; the number of hours a day and the number of days a week that a doctor is to be available; the requirement that a suitable vehicle and driver, provided by the employer, must be available for emergencies; the types of medicine to be stocked and the hours a pharmacy is to be open; regular arrangements for the transport of pregnant women to the nearest maternity facility for prenatal and postnatal care; a requirement that a professional nurse and a professional midwife must always be present on the estate; and provision for two union officers who "will aid in improving the medical service with their opinions and suggestions".

In almost all these agreements these services are provided without charge to the workers or members of their families.

Education of children

As with medical facilities, so with educational facilities. In developed countries the children of agricultural workers go to schools provided by the State; in many developing countries there are no, or very few, schools or teachers in rural areas. In such a situation the rural workers' organisations, particularly in the plantation sector, attempt to negotiate the provision of educational facilities by the employer; or, where the law requires the plantation employer to provide such services, to negotiate a higher standard and amount than the law requires.

In one example the employer is required to pay all expenses in maintaining a school to provide six years of education for the children of all workers; to hire an additional teacher to handle the overcrowding in the first form; to construct an annex to the existing school (built earlier by the employer on the estate) to be used as a classroom for the new first form; to construct four modern toilets in the school; and to construct another annex to serve as an office for the school.

There are several national-level agreements in developing countries, negotiated on an industry-wide basis, which require the employers' association to pay for a specified number of scholarships for advanced education for workers' children. One example provides for 24 scholarships each year to the national university, covering all expenses, including travel and clothing allowances. These are general scholarships—the students may choose their field of study. There are also examples of industrial scholarships negotiated at the estate level; in one case, a scholarship is to be paid for by the employer "for studies related to the sugar industry"—the grant is for eight years, the last five of which are spent at university. In all cases, scholarships are awarded either by a union committee or by a joint committee.

Consumer shops

Because some rural wage earners live in isolated areas and because employers or merchants may charge high prices for the goods the workers require, some agreements contain clauses aimed at furthering the interests of the workers in this respect. Rural wage earners' organisations adopt two different methods to tackle this problem. Some agreements, generally for one employer, require the employer to operate a non-profit store (in reality it runs at a loss). The employer is required to sell a specified list of articles at cost (based on the wholesale price at the nearest large city); he has to provide the building and cannot add to the price the costs of the workers employed to run the shop, of the transport of the goods or of the credit he extends to the workers.

On the other hand, another national agreement on an industry-wide basis takes the opposite position. No employer, directly or indirectly, can be associated with any shop on or near his estate which sells "articles of first necessity"; and, if his estate is more than 5 kilometres from an established public market, the employer must set aside land next to the workers' housing, where a free public market may be held, and erect stalls without charge. Moreover, if the workers form a consumer co-operative or a union store, the employer is obliged to loan to that co-operative or store a specified sum of money, depending on the amount of his annual production, to assist in starting up the establishment, and to provide free accommodation—or, if he is unable to do this, to provide a specified monthly cash subsidy to cover rent elsewhere.

Land for food production

A few agreements, usually negotiated with a single employer, provide for a specified area of land to be set aside, on which workers can grow vegetables for their own consumption.

Social and recreational provisions

Some collective agreements from the plantation sector require that the employer shall provide such facilities as a playground and equipment for the estate; a television set in each division; a cemetery; a social building and union office; and clothing and equipment for a football team or for other sports.

Seasonal wage earners

The interests of members who are seasonal workers call for special provisions, but not all collective agreements cater for these members. Arrangements concerning the entitlement of seasonal workers to benefits such as paid annual leave, sick leave and bonus participation vary considerably. In fact, in some agreements the union is not "recognised" [1] as repre-

---

[1] The definition of the scope of "recognition" (by the employer of the union's right to represent and bargain for the workers) is normally dealt with in the collective agreement itself, but in some cases a separate "recognition" agreement may be negotiated between the employer and the union.

senting seasonal workers. In others the exclusion of seasonal workers from the negotiated benefits results from the requirement that workers must have given one or two full years of service in order to be eligible, or that eligibility is restricted to hourly, daily and monthly paid workers when all the seasonal workers are on piece rates.

However, some organisations have negotiated agreements which provide that one or more of the benefits received by the permanent workers shall also be available to seasonal workers who work for a full season. In one such case seasonal workers are entitled to one week holiday with pay if they work not less than 75 per cent of the days on which work is available for them during the "crop season"; the permanent workers are entitled to two weeks if they work the whole year.

In some countries, by law, the organisations are recognised as representing all agricultural wage earners—permanent, permanent seasonal and temporary seasonal. In agreements negotiated under these conditions the seasonal and temporary workers receive the same benefits as the permanent workers, on a percentage basis of the days actually worked. In some cases this arrangement is secured through a kind of "insurance" fund: the employer pays various percentages of the wages of all workers into separate funds for annual leave, sick leave and for pensions and severance pay.

The housing provided for seasonal and temporary workers is another interest which is covered in some agreements. Generally, the agreement refers to "workers without families", but this really means workers who do not have their families with them because their work is seasonal only. As in the case of housing for permanent workers, the agreements require the construction of housing of a specified standard; most seek to abolish dormitory or compound-type accommodation and specify housing of no more than three workers to one room and greatly improved sanitary facilities.

Questions and points for discussion

1. What is the legal position in your country concerning the right of organisations of rural wage earners to bargain collectively for their members? Are seasonal wage earners covered by these provisions?

2. Is there a national collective agreement for rural wage earners in your country? Or a number of local agreements? Or both?

3. Is there a minimum wage for rural wage earners in your country? If so, are the wages and conditions in the collective agreement(s) better than those provided for by the minimum wage legislation?

4. What are the items covered by the collective agreement(s)? Are there other interests of rural wage earners which you feel should be covered by the agreement(s)? Are there other provisions besides those mentioned in this chapter?

Pressure-group activities for rural wage earners

11

In Chapter 10 we looked at one of the first kinds of service that a union for wage earners will normally seek to provide for its members: furthering and defending their interests by representation through bargaining activities. Here we investigate a different type of traditional trade union service: representation through pressure-group activities.

Pressure-group activities

Rural wage earners have interests which require furthering and defending not only vis-à-vis their employer but also within the economic, political and social life of the society and country in which they live. Rural wage earners' organisations seek to advance such interests through "pressure-group" activities: in other words, by presenting the members' interests to government, to political parties and to society as a whole with as much force as possible.

National policy and legislation

The interests of rural wage earners which are furthered and defended by their organisations through the policy-making and legislative processes of government are as varied and broad as the powers and responsibilities of government itself. The following are some examples of interests that rural wage earners' organisations are constantly representing at the national level on behalf of their members.

Trade union rights

Before they can become effective and continuing pressure groups, rural wage earners' organisations must have the legal right to exist. In other words, a law must be passed to allow them to register as workers' organisations. Once established, they may also feel the need for legal measures placing an obligation on the employers to recognise collective bargaining, to negotiate and to refrain from acts of anti-union discrimination. These are fundamental issues which are vital to the interests of rural workers and concerning which, generally in concert with the national trade union centre, rural wage earners' organisations will use pressure-group activities to obtain action on the part of the national legislature.

Minimum wages

Rural wage earners' organisations in most countries strive to have a minimum agricultural wage established by law, and to set that minimum as high as possible. Once achieved, a minimum wage is important in several ways: it creates a "floor" for agricultural wages, and the organisation can then (if it is strong enough) negotiate collective agreements with the employers for higher wages; it establishes a floor below which wages cannot fall during hard economic times (unless there is a change in the law); and it can bring about an increase in the wages of unorganised workers, which not only helps them but in the long run also helps those who are organised.

In some countries a new organisation may not be able to negotiate with the employers for a wage higher than the legal minimum. Where this is the case, and the minimum wage is actually determined by the government, pressure-group activities directed at the general public and political parties and/or government and aiming at increasing the minimum agricultural wage become even more important. Where there is a wages board or council and the organisation feels that its bargaining representations are not being taken sufficiently into account by the employers' representatives and the government appointees on that body, it may well feel obliged to undertake pressure-group activities to create a climate of public opinion in support of the fixing of as high a minimum wage as possible by the council, and of the government's confirming it as legally operative.

Hours

Everything we have said about wages applies also to hours of work. Hours worked affect both "wages" (in the sense of income received for each hour worked) and "income" (in the sense of the sum of money taken home by the worker). If daily or weekly wages are not changed when the number of hours worked is reduced, the "wages" earned for each hour of work rise; if the wages for each hour are unchanged but a worker is paid "time-and-a-half" for those hours worked over x hours each day or y hours each week, the "income" of the worker is increased. And so, for the same reasons as those invoked for minimum wages, rural wage earners' organisations strive for national legislation which establishes as low a number of daily or weekly hours of work as possible, and as high a "premium" pay as possible when those hours are exceeded. A strong organisation in a healthy economy may then negotiate even better terms through collective bargaining with the employers.

Health and safety

The need for rural wage earners' organisations to further and defend the interests of their members as regards health and safety in their work has always been important. Increasing mechanisation in agriculture, the likelihood and indeed the actual incidence of workers losing limbs, eyes and lives have multiplied the activities of rural wage earners' organisations in this field. They have always been much concerned by the use of chemicals in agriculture, which in recent years has increased tremendously in terms of amounts, varieties and danger to both human beings and farm and wild animals. Many have proved to be highly toxic and all are foreign substances as far as the skin, eyes, nervous system and digestive tract are concerned. Public support can be aroused to secure minimum health and safety standards by law in this field. Rural wage earners' organisations are advancing this interest of their members by publicising research carried out by institutes, by government health agencies and by the organisations themselves.

Inflation/recession

Few, if any, governments in the world today do not at least seek to influence either prices or wages (or both) by their policies or actions, whether real or threatened. What this means to agricultural wage earners is that governments do affect their "real wages"—that is, what they are able to buy with the money they take home from their work. If the prices the members are paying for food, clothing, housing and other basic items are rising faster than the money wages members take home, their "real wages" are falling. Governments generally have a wage/price policy or policies aimed at preventing or curbing inflation (prolonged sharp increases in the cost of living) and at preventing or correcting recessions (prolonged declines in economic activity and in employment). It is obvious that both these situations are of great economic interest to agricultural workers and that they wish their organisation to represent their interests when policies are formulated or action taken by their government. This is a pressure-group activity which the rural wage earners' organisation will normally undertake both individually and in concert with other workers' unions through the national centre to which it is affiliated.

Housing

The quality, availability, price and rents of housing for rural wage earners and their families are important interests of the members and often receive attention from their organisation. In the plantation sector housing is very frequently a subject of collective bargaining, since so many workers and their families live in employer-provided housing on the plantation itself. In some parts of Europe there are also "tied cottages" (houses owned by the employer and in which the worker lives) which are let often at a low rent or free of charge for as long as the employment lasts; however, when the job is at an end, for whatever reason, the worker has to leave the house. In both these cases the organisations press for national legislation setting down minimum standards for employer-provided housing (for instance, on the size and number of rooms for each family, the type and quality of construction, the provision of utilities and sanitation facilities, and maintenance and repair) and, in the case of tied cottages, providing the worker with reasonable security of tenure.

In addition, rural wage earners' organisations attempt to influence national policy as regards the government's housing programme (availability of government or government-subsidised housing or of schemes to stimulate the construction of housing in the rural areas, either for rent or for purchase). These activities further the interests both of rural wage earners who do not live in employer-provided housing and of those who do.

Medical facilities and services

In developed countries rural wage earners' organisations represent the needs of their members in this matter by seeking to influence legislation and policy in order to ensure the presence of adequate medical facilities and services in the rural sector. These organisations are also interested in the cost of the service to the members, whether that cost is in the form of government taxes, insurance premiums or private payments. Ultimately it is the worker who pays for the service; even when it is "free" or "paid by the employer", the amount paid by the employer is at least theoretically available to be negotiated as additional cash wages.

In developing countries, as we have seen, organisations in the plantation sector seek to meet this need of the membership through collective bargaining. But here also they press the government for improved legal minimum standards at the place of employment and for the presence of more medical facilities and services: the deliberate allocation of funds and medical personnel for those rural areas where there is little or no service at the moment.

Education

As observed earlier, educational facilities and services for the children of members are often a matter for collective bargaining in the plantation sector. But rural wage earners' organisations in both developing and developed countries represent this important interest of the members whenever policies, decisions or actions are pending at the national, regional or local levels regarding the availability, type and quality of education for the families of their members. "More schools", "better schools", "more advanced schools" in the rural area—these are some of the cries of rural wage earners' organisations to the public and to the appropriate authorities through pressure-group activities in representing this interest of the members.

Agricultural policies

The standard of living of the agricultural worker is directly related to the prosperity of the agricultural sector, and in almost all countries that prosperity is directly or indirectly influenced by government policies. Thus an important need of the members of rural wage earners' organisations is to try to ensure that the industry is in a position both to pay a decent wage and to provide adequate employment opportunities. An important pressure-group activity for rural wage earners' organisations is to seek to influence governments and political parties on the physical, legal, fiscal and administrative policies and actions which can affect the well-being of the agricultural sector as a whole, and in particular the activity on which the organisation's members are employed.

Quality of rural life

Agricultural, industrial and urban unions represent their membership in the legislative and policy-making processes on a broad range of interests, for example civil rights, consumer affairs and ecology. In addition, just as industrial and urban unions are active in matters concerning "urban affairs", so rural wage earners' organisations raise issues affecting "rural affairs"—the quality of life in the rural sector. Rural housing, medical services and educational facilities have already been discussed. Rural wage earners' organisations are also involved in campaigns to improve many other aspects of rural life: more cultural activities; more and cheaper transport services, both within the rural sector and to the urban areas; more sports activities; more and better roads; and more and cheaper distribution of utilities.

National and local administration

Important interests of rural wage earners are affected not only by national policy and legislation but also by administration or the lack of it. Most national legislation sets out only very broad outlines of policy, and the interpretation and implementation of the legislation leaves considerable decision-making responsibility to administrators at various levels. Rural wage earners' organisations identify these centres of decision and represent their members' interests. In this age of economic and social planning by governments, much that affects the interests of agricultural workers is found in "plans"; the organisations therefore seek representation in some form at all levels on all appropriate governmental, semi-governmental or "mixed" commissions, boards, institutes or other bodies. The organisation wants to be present to the greatest extent possible when the plans and decisions are made.

Moreover, the gains made through legislation on such matters as minimum wages, health and safety standards, child labour laws and minimum housing standards can be lost through lack of proper enforcement. The organisation, by providing information to its members, keeps them advised of their rights and of the law. Members, officials and officers, directly or indirectly, can help to "police" the enforcement and administration of the law at the local level. This is true in all countries, but in developing countries in particular there are rarely enough government inspectors because of the government's lack of resources; in these situations the organisation's officials and officers often become the only "inspectors", reporting violations through the organisation to the government department concerned.

Ability of the organisation to influence and to represent

The ability of a rural workers' organisation to further and defend the members' interests effectively in the political and social life of the country depends on the strength of the organisation—on the number of its dues-paying members and on the ability of the elected leadership of the organisation. Governments, political parties and society as a whole are able to count; if the membership of the organisation is low when expressed as a percentage of the total number of rural wage earners in the country, the influence of the organisation will be low. Able leaders can conceivably exert somewhat more influence than the number of members justifies, but not very much more. If the percentage of actual members to potential members is high—it really needs to be 50 per cent or more—government, political parties and society as a whole accept the organisation as the genuine "voice" of the agricultural wage earners, and the organisation is thus in a position to represent the interests of its members effectively at the national level. The first step towards effective representation, therefore, is the organisation of all agricultural wage earners at the local level.

But the recognition of the organisation as the voice of the agricultural wage earners only opens the way towards the effective representation of the members' interests. Representation is a matter of research, planning, publicity and a great deal of hard work. The national leadership must carefully select and plan the methods to be used in influencing national policy measures and legislation furthering the interests of rural wage earners. The range of methods is very wide, particularly as regards the relationship of the organisation with government and political parties. Generally (although there are some exceptions) rural wage earners' organisations have the same relationship with government and political parties and use the same methods to influence national policy measures and legislation as their "sister"[1] unions of workers in other occupations in the same country. The range of relationships between an organisation and a party extends from, at one extreme, the organisation's being closely allied to or even a part of a political party, to the case in which there is no relationship with or support for any party—the organisation supports or opposes individual candidates, irrespective of party, in the light of a candidate's personal public record as it relates to those issues of interest to agricultural workers. Similarly, with regard to union officers and officials who seek election to public office (for example, on local authorities or in the national legislature), in some unions this practice is actively encouraged,

---

[1] In many countries trade unionists refer to one another as "brother" and "sister" and union members extend to one another "fraternal" greetings. They also refer to another union as a "sister" organisation.

but in others the officer or official must resign his post if he becomes a candidate for public office. These are the extreme positions; there are many intervening degrees.[1]

The actual influence that the organisation wields through its pressure-group activities on behalf of agricultural wage earners—assuming strength of numbers and ability of leaders—largely depends on both officials and officers putting in hard work and long hours. This applies to the national, regional and local levels; but it is particularly true as regards volunteer officers at the local and regional levels who, in addition to working a full day and week as agricultural wage earners, must spend many hours preparing for and attending local and regional meetings of commissions, boards and institutes.

Questions and points for discussion

1. If there is a national organisation of rural wage earners in your country, identify the interests of the membership that it is furthering and defending through pressure-group activities, and the methods used. Are there any additional interests of the members which you feel could be furthered in this way? What are they, and what methods would you suggest should be used?

2. If there is no national organisation of rural wage earners in your country, identify the first three interests of rural wage earners which you feel would need to be furthered and defended if one were formed. Assume that you are an official of that newly formed union; how would you recommend that the union should tackle the three interests you have selected?

---

[1] In this connection it is useful to refer again to the principle covered by the ILO resolution concerning the independence of the trade union movement (p. 56), in which it was stressed that governments "should not attempt to transform the trade union movement into an instrument for the pursuance of political aims, nor should they attempt to interfere with the normal functions of a trade union movement...".

Other services for rural wage earners

12

As well as negotiations and pressure-group activities, a rural workers' organisation may provide a number of other services for its members. The range of these services is as wide as that of the members' needs. Here we shall review some of the traditional types of union service and then look at some special services designed to meet the special needs of the rural wage earner.

Union cash benefits

Union cash benefits are those payments made by the union to members (or their families) who may be in financial difficulties. Such payments exemplify the principle of "mutual protection" with which workers' organisations in every industry have always been concerned. One early example of mutual protection was the death benefit to which a worker became entitled on joining a union, and to provide which a percentage of the dues paid to the organisation was set aside in a reserve fund, to be used for making lump-sum payments to the families of any members who died. Many rural wage earners' organisations provide this service for their members. Others, whilst not providing cash benefits themselves, seek to obtain them for the widows and children of deceased members through pressure-group activities aimed at extending the provisions of the national social security scheme as regards death benefits to cover the survivors of agricultural workers. Others again adopt a third method, and negotiate for the payment of lump-sum benefits by the employer directly or for the establishment of an insurance scheme for this purpose, with the employer paying all or part of the premiums. Many organisations follow more than one of these methods; a few follow all three.

Another important benefit of the "mutual protection" type also dates from the earliest days of the trade union movement. This is strike benefit. Again, a percentage of the union's income from the members is set aside in a reserve fund to be used for payments to members on strike. In some unions there are two dues: one is paid into the general fund, and the other (the strike benefit dues) is paid into a strike fund, the moneys of which can be used only for the payment of strike benefit. The double-dues system has the advantage that it clearly separates, in the minds of members, the money that they are contributing for the expenses of their organisation and the money that, in effect, they are putting aside to be returned to them if they find themselves without income because of a strike or lock-out. A second advantage is that if over a long period there are no strikes and if it is considered that there is enough money in the strike fund, the payment of the strike benefit dues may be temporarily suspended.

Since strike action, as a means of furthering and defending the interests of the members, is normally taken only when all else has failed, a strike fund represents an important service to the membership. It is even possible that the existence of a large strike fund may make a strike unnecessary—the employer may well concede more of the workers' claims if he realises that the workers are financially capable of sustaining an effective strike. But in many countries, particularly in developing countries, rural wage earners' organisations do not have a strike fund because all the income they receive from members is absorbed in meeting the costs of organising on a national basis and of providing services to meet other immediate needs of members.

Legal services

All unions require legal advice and services from time to time—for matters requiring court action, for the phrasing of proposed legislation, for legal interpretations of laws, decrees or collective agreements, and so on. Many unions also provide a free legal service to their members in matters which are related to their work or in defence of their rights as workers—for instance, legal processes or litigation related to discharge, work-related accidents or sickness, denial of benefits, incorrect pay, and so on. Some organisations provide semi-legal services by, for example, assisting members to process benefit claims (sickness, accident, retirement, unemployment) with the government and/or employer or to obtain work permits and/or citizenship in those countries where a significant percentage of the rural workers come from another country.

A few organisations are able to provide personal legal services to members at a fee much lower than that normally charged. They do so by making an arrangement with the lawyers whom the organisation employs or retains for its own legal needs.

Workers' information and educational activities

All rural wage earners' organisations provide information and educational activities as a service to members. The variety and number of these activities depend on the stage of development of the organisation, the resources available to it and the particular needs of the members.

Organisation newspaper

One of the most effective ways in which a rural wage earners' organisation can further and defend the interests of its members is by providing regular information which keeps members informed of their rights under the collective agreement and under the laws of their country; of the organisation's activities in seeking changes in the collective agreement and changes in national policy and legislation; and of events and circumstances which may further or threaten their interests. Most rural wage earners' organisations begin some form of regular written communication to the members at an early stage of their development. It may be no more than a duplicated one-sheet monthly "newsletter" sent to the principal local officer to be read to the membership; or it may be a monthly newspaper or magazine sent to each member. Figure 2, showing some typical communication flows, serves as a reminder that, whilst the organisation has to provide an information service *to* the members, it must, if it is to be effective, have adequate and well established means and procedures through which information and views *from* the members can effectively reach the administration.

Trade union (workers') education

Most rural wage earners' organisations have some form of workers' education programme, however sporadic, for their officers and officials. These programmes range from short seminars or evening courses, conducted with the help of the national trade union centre or an international workers' organisation, to more formal and lengthy educational courses on a full-time basis. The subjects covered in these courses are chosen to meet the most urgent needs of the participants at the time. Many organisations also run short trade union courses for members at the local level; these briefly cover all aspects of agrarian trade unionism and particularly the rights and responsibilities of the members. Some organisations have more advanced courses which are intended to develop future leaders. However, whatever type of course is organised, it is important to realise that what is offered is *workers'* education—the education of workers about matters affecting workers and workers' organisations, carried out by and through workers' organisations and (wherever possible) by workers themselves.[1]

It is also important to realise that, especially in the rural sector, workers' education activities do not necessarily have to be approached in a sophisticated manner; indeed, it is often the case that the simpler the approach, the

---

[1] For a comprehensive treatment of workers' education, see ILO: *Workers' education and its techniques: A workers' education manual* (Geneva, 1976) and the working paper submitted to the Symposium on Workers' Education Methods and Techniques for Rural Workers and Their Organisations, op. cit.

more likely it is that the desired ends will be achieved. If a group of rural wage earners are brought together in a formal education setting, such as a classroom or lecture hall, and faced with a professional teacher (however good and understanding he may be), the utter strangeness of the environment is immediately a barrier to their obtaining the maximum benefit from the educational activity. If, on the other hand, they meet in a member's home or in the local meeting-place (even if this is in the open air), and the "educator" is an official or officer of their own or another workers' organisation, the atmosphere is one in which they feel more comfortable and in which they are therefore more likely to derive the maximum benefit from the activity. Except for the more advanced levels of workers' education and training carried out by well established and financially secure organisations, this second approach is the one which is followed by the majority of rural wage earners' organisations.

The educational activities have to be adjusted to the means at an organisation's disposal and to the time at the members' disposal—paid educational leave is the exception rather than the rule amongst rural wage earners, and at certain times of the year their work leaves them with very little spare time. Consequently, evening or weekend courses or classes are confined to the "slack" seasons and, because of transport problems and costs, are organised on a local basis. In order to keep down costs, more than one organisation runs week-end courses to which the participants bring their own food, which they cook themselves.

However, even with this very simple approach, educational activities are bound to cost the organisation something, and if any kind of methodical programme for the whole organisation is envisaged—and unless it is, the vital educational activities are unlikely to be undertaken—the organisation must set aside a certain sum of money for this purpose each year. This is an aspect of management which does not always receive the attention that it should.

Special services to meet members' needs [1]

In addition to the more traditional services provided by rural wage earners' organisations for their members (collective bargaining, pressure-group activities, cash benefits, legal assistance, and so forth), many organisations are developing other services to meet the special needs of their members. Here we shall examine only eight broad types of such services; but in practice, as we have already observed with regard to traditional services, the range and variety of services that are being, or could be, or should be provided is as wide as the range of special needs of rural wage earners and their families.

Unemployment

As well as fighting unemployment and its effects through collective bargaining and pressure-group activities for full employment policies and

---

[1] A fuller treatment of these services is given in ILO: *Special services of rural workers' organisations* (Geneva, 1978).

social security legislation, a few rural wage earners' organisations, when faced with heavy unemployment among their members, have started new services and programmes to alleviate this serious problem. To give just one example, a plantation union in a developing country has been very active in this field because its members are faced with increasing unemployment as a result of a number of factors: introduction of more sophisticated technology, which has resulted in 16 per cent fewer workers being needed to tap the same acreage of rubber trees; diversification of agriculture, with some land being diverted from rubber to oil palm cultivation, which requires a 50 per cent lower input of labour; the dividing up of large estates; and the high birth rate among workers on plantations.

This organisation has introduced various programmes over the years to combat unemployment among its members. In conjunction with the local authorities and a private institution, it has established a vocational training institute where plantation workers are trained in other occupations so that they may take technical jobs in other industries. To help to create new jobs, the organisation, together with other unions, was instrumental in establishing a workers' bank, with the savings of all categories of worker being loaned to job-creating industries. The organisation has also formed a trading corporation through which, with and without collaboration, it has started enterprises to provide new jobs in the plantation areas. The biggest such enterprise to date is a joint venture with a local authority and a private company to establish a textile mill which, when fully operational, will provide 2,000 new jobs. This organisation's goal is to set up at least two new job-creating enterprises in each region where there are unemployed plantation workers.

To fight the loss of plantation jobs caused by the dividing up of plantations, the organisation, through its trading corporation, has bought one 2,000-acre plantation.[1] The organisation has also formed a national multi-purpose society through which it plans to start a housing programme, cottage industries and land settlement schemes—all in areas where there is plantation unemployment. This society has purchased a 500-acre estate to launch these programmes, which will absorb a significant portion of the unemployed on adjacent plantations.

To reduce unemployment attributable to the high birth rate in the plantation sector, the organisation conducts courses in family planning throughout the sector under its educational programme.[2]

---

[1] The reader may ask how an organisation negotiates wages and conditions of work when it is itself the employer. In fact, it does not. What it does is to hire a management company to run the plantation. The management company then signs the same collective agreement as the organisation has negotiated with the employers' association.

[2] In Chapter 8 we noted that most rural workers' organisations that are providing a worthwhile service to the members apply dues rates of about 2 per cent of the income of the lowest-paid members. This is the case as regards this organisation, and others like it, which are so active in servicing the special needs of their members. The dues rates applied average only slightly less than 2 per cent of members' wages; moreover, in this particular case a number of the organisation's more important activities have been financed by collections and levies from members over and above the normal union dues.

Illiteracy

In countries or localities with a high illiteracy rate in rural areas, many rural wage earners' organisations are active in servicing the need of members and their families for literacy training. As well as attacking this problem through representation to employers and government, a number of organisations are operating literacy training schemes specifically for members and their adult relatives. Some are doing so alone, others in conjunction with government and/or institutions. Some organisations have even been able greatly to increase the effectiveness of literacy training by incorporating into the lessons material on the interests and needs of the workers—a form of functional literacy training—and thus providing increased motivation. Depending on the needs of the membership and the size of the organisation, these programmes may serve as few as 100 members a year or, as in one example, train in one year as many as 1,500 members and their adult relatives to read and write.

Special needs of youth

The interest of members in the education and future employment prospects of their children gives rise to many activities by rural wage earners' organisations. In developed countries the organisations represent this interest during the political and social decision-making processes. In the plantation sector they also do so during negotiations with the employer. Some organisations in developing countries attack the problem directly through union-sponsored programmes and schemes, either alone or jointly with government and/or institutions.

Several rural wage earners' organisations provide important educational programmes for members' children. In one case the organisation spends 23 per cent of its income and 5 per cent of the income of its associated co-operative-type schemes on educational programmes. The law in the country in question requires plantation employers to provide education only for the first three years of schooling. The organisation, as part of its own educational project, brought together a number of interested members who were also fathers in order to develop a programme, and negotiated with the employers for the necessary buildings on the various plantations. Working with the ministry of education, this union-sponsored programme now has 14 such schools, providing education from the first-form to the sixth-form levels. As the secondary schools of the area were educationally inefficient and were charging exorbitant fees, the organisation's educational scheme took over a school which had financial problems, employed only fully qualified teachers and lowered the fees to about 70 per cent of the previous rates: it has since added a full physics and chemistry laboratory and an extension for vocational training. Today, this school has over 1,000 students and the quality of the other schools in the area has been raised to compete with it, to the benefit of the whole community. The organisation's educational scheme pays the fees of one child for members who have two or more children at the school, while members receiving low wages pay only half fees for their children.

Special needs of women

Women, as agricultural workers and union members in some situations, and as dependent wives and daughters of members in other situations, have special problems and interests. Some unions have successfully fought for facilities to be provided by the employer and/or government for the children of working mothers. In other countries the unions themselves have developed and operate "day care centres" as part of their services to members. Under these programmes, a working mother pays a very low fee for placing her children in the centre, where the children are looked after by trained personnel and receive food, medical attention and education while the mother works.

Many rural wage earners' organisations, acting alone or jointly with others, provide family planning information and educational programmes. Literacy programmes are also designed for the wives of members. Several organisations provide educational programmes on family health and nutrition, particularly in areas where the traditional foods have been found to be in some way deficient for the development of the children or the general health of the family.

Consumer co-operative-type activities

As noted earlier, rural wage earners' organisations further and defend the interests of their members as consumers by representation to government for the control or limitation of increases in the prices of at least the basic necessities of life. In addition, unions in both developed and developing countries have for many years worked closely with the consumer co-operative movement as another way of securing higher "real wages"—that is, by eliminating the profits of the middle men. In some countries there is no strong co-operative movement, particularly in the rural areas. Many rural wage earners' organisations have started "union co-operatives" (co-operatives whose membership is limited to union members) or, where the laws governing the registration of co-operatives do not permit this type of organisation,[1] have

---

[1] A trade union is by nature a "closed" association, in that it exists to serve the interests of a defined group of workers. Not anyone can be a member: only those who satisfy the conditions of membership as set out in the union rules may join. On the other hand, a fundamental principle of the co-operative movements in many countries is that they shall be "open" societies: that is, anyone who wishes to become a member of the co-operative may do so. Where this principle is also laid down in a country's legislation on co-operatives, a workers' organisation cannot establish a registered co-operative and at the same time restrict the membership and benefits of that co-operative to the organisation's members. Occasionally unions do establish co-operatives which are open to all, but naturally they generally seek to find ways and means of providing this special service in such a way that it is available only to members of the union. Where the union decides upon (and the law allows) the establishment of a formal co-operative, the latter has all the

formed union-owned "enterprises", "stores" or "trading corporations", which are operated on a non-profit-making basis. Rural wage earners' organisations have undertaken this type of service for their members where they have been unable to persuade governments to adopt legislation and policies controlling the price of basic necessities and where the charges of the middle men and merchants have been high.

In developing countries these union-run consumer co-operatives or schemes tend to concentrate on basic food and household needs such as maize, flour, rice, salt , sugar, cooking oil, meat, milk, eggs, matches, charcoal, fuel oil, stoves, soap, and so on. Some are able greatly to expand the variety of items offered as they gain in experience and financial strength. The co-operatives sell to all union members, whether or not they are members of the co-operative or enterprise. When first started in an area, these schemes have lowered prices by between 15 per cent and as much as 50 per cent on some items. The competition soon forces the local merchants to lower their prices too, and all consumers in the area benefit from the scheme. Union members may in addition receive a discount on their purchases, and if they are shareholders in the co-operative they may also receive interest on their investment.

Several of these consumer co-operatives own their own transport, so that they can buy items in large quantities as close to their place of origin as possible and also take them to the most remote areas in which their members live, where prices tend to be highest.

Savings and loans schemes

Rural wage earners' organisations in many countries have helped to foster credit unions; in other countries they have developed union-operated savings and loans activities. In the remote rural areas in many countries money-lenders often operate without legal restriction on the rates of interest they charge; in others there is no effective administration of such laws as may exist. Past cases of exorbitant interest rates may be quoted in areas where unions have subsequently developed savings and loans schemes. To take just one example: if a worker borrowed NU 100, he had to sign a document saying that he had borrowed and received NU 200—on which the interest could be as much as 25 per cent a week.

When establishing a savings and loan scheme, a union has first to organise a campaign of information and education, through its newsletter and through meetings, on the idea and value of regular savings. These campaigns are often tied to slogans. The union itself makes a large contribution to the scheme by

---

characteristics of operation, management and membership control of the co-operatives of that country. If, on the other hand, the union is unable, or does not wish, to establish a formal co-operative, it may nevertheless undertake a co-operative-type activity itself, based on its own structure and membership. Whilst the aim of both methods is the same—to provide a special service to members—the operational principles differ greatly.

For further information on the internationally agreed norms relating to co-operatives, see the ILO's Co-operatives (Developing Countries) Recommendation, 1966 (No. 127).

Rural workers' organisations have raised housing standards for their members (above)

Plantation workers hold a meeting to discuss strike action (below)

meeting the initial costs related to education, organisation, guidance, equipment and office space. When sufficient savings have been accumulated it is not difficult to lend the money because the rate of interest is generally 1 per cent a month on the balance of the loan—considerably lower than the rates charged by local money-lenders. Several schemes operated by rural wage earners' organisations are loaning large sums to members, and the number of such schemes continues to grow.

Rural wage earners' organisations have also joined with other unions in some countries to sponsor jointly the establishment and development of national workers' banks to serve the same and wider purposes.

Housing needs

A few rural wage earners' organisations have developed housing schemes of their own, besides attacking this problem through collective bargaining or through representation during the national legislative and policy-making process. Union-operated housing schemes are a relatively new form of special service to members, but sufficient experience has now been gained to show that they can be operated successfully. Because assistance from banks and government are needed, particularly in the early stages, such schemes require a union strong in administrative experience and with a successful record in operating other schemes for the members. In one example, a union starting a housing scheme managed to persuade the government to donate some land; a cash donation was received from an organisation of businessmen and merchants in the town to cover the cost of installing roads, footpaths, water and other services; and an institution donated technical assistance.[1] The union then secured a commitment from banks for loans (mortgages) for members who wished to buy houses, and contracted for the building of some 300 dwelling places. The members pay back the loan over 10 to 24 years, depending on the payment plan they choose, at an interest rate of 6 per cent a year on the outstanding balance. This project has grown and a total of over 1,000 houses have now been constructed, and bought by members.

Health care needs

Most rural wage earners' organisations in developed countries press the health care needs of the members and their families through pressure-group activities aimed at introducing legislation and policies that make health care a part of social security and that allocate sufficient medical installations and personnel to the rural areas. In developing countries rural wage earners' organisations are often able, through collective bargaining, to negotiate with the employers for better health care for their members than exists under social

---

[1] It should be emphasised that the ability of a rural wage earners' organisation to obtain donations in cash, in kind and in technical assistance from other sectors of society for such projects depends entirely on society's assessment of the organisation's strength and of the ability of the leadership.

The "identity card" enables a rural worker to participate
in and benefit from his organisation's activities
and services

security. This is particularly true in the plantation sector. However, situations do arise where the organisations are unable to obtain health care services for their members by these traditional methods. This is especially so where a large percentage of the members (50 per cent and over) are not only seasonal workers but also migrant workers. In such a situation some organisations are turning to co-operative-type health care schemes operated by the organisation to service the very serious needs of their members. The development of this type of direct servicing is very recent, but in one example a rural wage earners' organisation negotiated a collective agreement with one large employer of migrant seasonal agricultural workers under which the employer pays a fixed amount for every hour worked by each worker to a "foundation" established by the organisation.[1] This foundation operates a health care scheme for the organisation's members. The plans call for the establishment of clinics, owned and operated by the health care scheme, which are staffed by doctors and other medical personnel who are employees of the scheme and who provide all local medical services to members and their families. In addition, this scheme also meets all the costs (including transport) if members or their families are sent by the clinics to hospitals in the cities.

Questions and points for discussion

1. Suppose that you were entrusted with the responsibility of arranging a series of workers' education meetings designed to assist local leaders of a rural wage earners' organisation to understand their role and responsibilities better. What physical arrangements would you make for the meetings (place, time, etc.)? Who would you expect to be the educator? What would be the main subjects you would expect to cover? Why?

2. Which workers' organisations that you know undertake workers' education activities as a service to members? Do those activities meet the basic needs of the members and the organisation?

3. Identify any special services that have been developed to meet the special needs of members in an organisation with which you are familiar. What methods have been used to implement those special services? Was outside finance required to start them? Have they remained under the control of the organisation?

4. If the members of that organisation have another pressing need for which a service ought to be provided, how would you recommend that the organisation should develop such a service? What would be the physical, financial and personnel requirements for setting up the service?

---

[1] This is another example of a union adopting a form of organisation that is legally recognised in its own country. A "foundation" in the country in question is a non-profit-making organisation which pays no taxes.

Pressure-group activities for self-employed rural workers 13

In Chapters 10 to 12 we examined the interests of the rural wage earners and saw how their organisations further and defend these interests. We noted that service to membership is the reason for the very existence of a workers' organisation, and that all the organisation's forces and activities are concentrated on providing services to meet the members' interests and needs.

In this chapter we shall consider some of the main interests and needs of self-employed rural workers and see how their organisations service these interests and needs.

Representation by collective bargaining?

It is true to say that the notion of representation by collective bargaining, that is, by negotiations between employers and workers' representatives, is not applicable as regards those rural workers who are self-employed, since they have no employer. In theory, sharecroppers and tenants might bargain collectively through their representatives with a landlord, but this is generally not feasible under the existing law and practice in most developing countries. Even if the laws were changed to give sharecroppers and tenants this trade union right in conformity with international labour standards, the cases where collective bargaining could be successfully used would still be few in number. Most landlords have only a few sharecroppers or tenants, and in any one country the sheer number of "collective agreements" to be negotiated with the landlords by the organisation, acting on behalf of all sharecroppers or tenants, would make it an impossible task. Furthermore, if it were necessary to negotiate individually, with one landlord at a time, the organisation would virtually be acting with "the feeble strength of one", in the sense that a landlord in a developing country could easily find new sharecroppers or tenants to replace any who sought to improve their lot through bargaining. In a situation in which 50 per cent or more of the sharecroppers and tenants in an area became organised, the organisation might perhaps be able to induce the landlords to send representatives to negotiate a collective agreement with its own representatives on matters concerning terms of tenancy and other conditions of interest to sharecroppers and tenants. But what sanction can the workers—the sharecroppers and tenants—operate? How real is the threat that they will withhold their labour if negotiations are not successful? In the case of wage earners, the possibility of a workers' strike is generally the factor that makes employers negotiate in earnest. If the sharecroppers and tenants withhold their labour—do not plant, cultivate or harvest at the appropriate time—they will lose all their income for a whole year! No strike fund could be developed that would meet the needs created by this situation. And the landlords know this—so no realistic pressure can be brought to bear on the landlords to bargain.

And what of the subsistence owner-occupier? He has no landlord with whom to attempt to bargain. And the landless labourer? He has no land about which to bargain.

At this point, many people (including some trade unionists) may say that if there is no employer with whom to bargain for better wages, hours and working conditions, there can be no union. This shows a deep misunderstanding of the *raison d'être* of a union, of a workers' organisation. Let us go back and look again at the definition of a rural workers' organisation: by a rural workers' organisation is meant the coming together of rural workers in an association established on a continuing and democratic basis, dependent on its own resources and independent of patronage, the purpose of which is to further and defend the interests of the members. A rural workers' organisation is a trade union or trade-union-type organisation of, for and by rural workers. There is no mention here of "employer", nor of "wages"—only of furthering and defending the interests of the rural worker members. Let us now go back and see again how "rural workers" are defined. We said that, first and foremost, they are workers; that they feed, house and clothe themselves and their families by their toil; and that those who are in any way employers are not considered to be rural workers. Sharecroppers, tenants and subsistence owner-occupiers are *workers,* and therefore an organisation of, for and by them that furthers and defends their interests is a union—a rural workers' union.

It is clear, however, that organisations of sharecroppers, tenants, subsistence owner-occupiers and landless labourers do not service the economic interests and needs of their members through "representation by collective bargaining". How, then, do they set about doing so?

Representation by pressure-group activities

In Chapter 11 we observed that rural wage earners have interests which require furthering and defending, not only vis-à-vis their employer but also within the economic, political and social life of the society and country in which they live. In the case of self-employed rural workers *all* their interests require furthering and defending within the political, economic and social life of their country. Representation by pressure-group activities is the principal reason for the existence of a peasant[1] organisation in developing countries—the peasant is calling for the reform of the society in which he lives.

The predominating economic interest of the rural wage earner is work. Unemployment, for whatever reason, is his biggest fear. The predominating economic interest of the self-employed rural worker is land. The lack or loss of land to work is his biggest fear. The rural wage earner wants higher wages and other economic benefits from the employer. The sharecropper, tenant or landless labourer wants land—land he owns himself. He wants the land that he is now working, or the land of some other landlord or of the State. The rural workers' organisation of which he is a member can very seldom "negotiate" that with anyone. In most developing countries, as far as the peasants' needs and interests in land are concerned, the peasant is ultimately seeking a restructuring of the economic, social and political life of the rural sector.

Agrarian reform

The peasant in developing countries is seeking reform—agrarian reform. In this section we describe what is meant by "land reform" and "agrarian reform"; look at statistics on the distribution of land in some developing countries; and indicate the need for reform to advance rural development.

Definitions

The nature of the reforms being sought by peasants in developing countries varies with the particular situation in which they find themselves in their own country. However, as the term is generally understood and as it is used here, "land reform" includes the reform of the tenure system and/or the abolition of landlordism, with land redistribution. The reform of the land tenure system includes, inter alia, the regulation or prohibition of crop sharing; security of tenure; the limitation of rent charges; and payment for improvements made by the tenant. "Land redistribution" is generally considered to express the concept of "land to the tiller"; it includes land consolidation, so that the tiller will become the owner of a "family-size" farm. Land belonging to the State can also be redistributed.

"Agrarian reform" or "integrated agrarian reform" covers land reform and the concept that reform limited to the mere transfer of land to those who till the soil is not sufficient and is meaningless if the necessary credit, technical assistance, markets and transport facilities are not introduced at the same time, so as to increase production and the value received by the peasants for

---

[1] In the literature dealing with rural workers the term "peasant" is applied to the self-employed rural worker, such as the sharecropper, tenant or small owner-occupier.

their production. Peasant organisations add a third element to their definition of agrarian reform: the participation of the peasants' representatives as an intrinsic part of, and indeed the basic step in, agrarian reform.[1]

Statistics from some developing countries

As we saw in Chapter 1, the agricultural population in most developing countries accounts for anything between 40 and 90 per cent of the total population. In many countries a large proportion of the land is owned by the few, and the masses work the land on a share, rental or wage basis. There are countries where a few hundred families, or no more than 2 per cent of the population, own 45 to 80 per cent of the land. In one geographical region, for example, estates of more than 1,000 hectares, although representing only 1.5 per cent of the total number of agricultural units, cover 64.9 per cent of the total area under cultivation; on the other hand, smallholdings of under 20 hectares account for 72.6 per cent of the total in terms of numbers, but occupy only 3.7 per cent of the land. The significance of these figures will be even more readily grasped if we compare the concentration of ownership with the distribution of manpower: in one country in that same region, for instance, small family holdings occupy only 5 per cent of the land but employ—or rather, underemploy—60 per cent of the working agricultural population, whereas the large estates cover 50 per cent of the land but provide employment for only 4.2 per cent of the agricultural labour force. In addition, it has been estimated that in seven countries in the region in question the large estates have only one-sixth of their land under cultivation.

Need for reform to advance economic development

The following two quotations are typical of current international thinking on agrarian reform.

There is no doubt about the view of the United Nations and its specialised agencies in regard to agrarian reform. . . . the General Assembly, ECOSOC, FAO[2] and ILO have recommended it as the foremost instrument of social justice, and a fundamental part of the strategy of economic development.

. . . .

Agrarian reform must be considered both as a starting-point and as an instrument for general economic development whose effects embrace the great mass of the population. Such development consists not only in increasing over-all income but essentially in transforming the people and redistributing economic, social and political power. Viewed thus from this dynamic standpoint, it helps to maintain socio-economic organisation properly geared to the requirements and aspirations of that mass and, hence, is an essential factor in creating and maintaining an egalitarian society.

---

[1] For a broad definition of agrarian reform see the resolution on agrarian reform, with particular reference to employment and social aspects, adopted by the International Labour Conference in 1965.

[2] ECOSOC: United Nations Economic and Social Council. FAO: Food and Agriculture Organisation of the United Nations.

These quotations are taken from the report of the FAO Special Committee on Agrarian Reform,[1] which also observed that it is difficult to imagine the achievement of agrarian reform and rural development without the effective participation of rural workers; and that such participation could not be achieved by individual peasants—they could not achieve genuine independence if they are not "associated". The Committee went on:

Association is a virtually irreplaceable instrument for disseminating technological progress and capitalising agriculture, and is essential for introducing "freedom of status", which no longer simply means breaking feudal patterns of land tenure but also acquiring the ability to help with the creation of a new structure, with the management of rural services and with the whole range of national policy and economy.

The association between agrarian reform and rural development is also stressed in the International Labour Code. The two are related in the Preambles of Convention No. 141 and of Recommendation No. 149;[2] rural development is specifically referred to in Article 5 and Paragraph 4 of the two instruments respectively; and the need for rural workers' organisations to be associated with rural development and the planning and implementation of agrarian reform is also specifically spelt out in Paragraph 12 of the Recommendation.

The members of the FAO Special Committee stated that their review of the status of agrarian reform in the world led them to the conclusion that agrarian reform implies, first and foremost, a political decision. They reasoned that the changing of the structure of land tenure (when accompanied or followed by other necessary measures such as the provision of a suitable infrastructure and adequate credit, storage, processing and marketing facilities) "promotes not only a redistribution of an income swelled by technical progress but also a fundamental alteration in the position of the existing social strata and hence, a redistribution of power". In the process the peasants become independent of the owners of land and are given a part in the running of the services of the agricultural sector and in rural development. Their participation also extends to the broader field of land-use planning, national planning and, in general, the country's whole policy. Acceptance of these consequences, said the Committee, "clearly implies taking a decision of a political nature, and the possibility of so doing depends in its turn on the attitude of the governing classes towards the need for change or, failing a positive attitude, on the influence that other social strata are capable of acquiring".

The process of redistributing land is obviously bound to provoke reactions from those who feel their interests are threatened. The matter was put plainly and succinctly by the Special Committee:

Clearly, the delay by some countries in implementing reform has given interests that feel themselves threatened by it time to organise themselves, sometimes in an

---

[1] FAO: *Report of the Special Committee on Agrarian Reform,* op. cit.

[2] See Appendix B.

atmosphere of growing intransigence which may lead to serious disturbances, as has occurred in the past. There is no hiding the fact that this attitude of a section of the land-owning classes and their political representatives magnifies the first and most formidable of the obstacles to reform, namely, the difficulty of taking a decision to undertake it or of not paralysing efforts already started.... Moreover, the strong inertia of unjust structures which impede development is not yet counterbalanced by a vigorous organisation of the peasant masses. These have not yet even acquired, in some cases, a clear awareness of what they should demand and obtain nor of the part they must play in the development process.

Peasant organisations and agrarian reform

Peasants in developing countries are not usually concerned with statistics and, although they may be patriotic, the economic development of their country is not their primary personal interest. Agrarian reform, for most of them, is a way out of their economic, social and political poverty; and, as has been said earlier, agrarian reform is the prime interest to be furthered and defended by their organisations. Here we examine the need for agrarian reform as seen by the peasants; how their organisations struggle for agrarian reform; and how they, through their organisations, participate in agrarian reform.

Need for reform: the peasants' view

In most countries where the need for agrarian reform is great, peasant pressure for land dominates the rural workers' organisations. The acquisition of land is the main objective which motivates hundreds of thousands of peasants to join local and national peasant organisations. Whilst it may appear that the landless or the land-hungry look to land reform as a means of ensuring their food and shelter, in reality they are seeking much more. To them, the ownership of land brings much more than wealth: it is for them the source of prestige, political power and social justice. It gives them the right to build their own houses in which to raise their families, and also the right to tax themselves in order to build a school or to provide other social services. Through owning land they acquire a wide range of rights which hitherto have always been the prerogative only of the large landowners.

Given the possibility of forming and joining rural workers' organisations, the peasants' demand for agrarian reform has been reflected in the programmes, literature and constitutions of their organisations. As a typical example, the constitution of one national rural workers' organisation includes among the objectives of the organisation the following:

— to defend constitutional democratic rule;

— to unify and direct organised collective action by the country's peasants and rural workers in defence of their economic and social interests;

— to fight for an agrarian reform that eliminates the system of large landed estates and replaces it by a total democratisation of all land holdings for the benefit of those who directly work the land;

— to work for the steady improvement of social legislation so as to increase the participation of peasants and rural workers in the enjoyment of the material wealth they help to create through their work;

— to work for the eradication of peasant compounds and for the provision for each family of a spacious and comfortable home that fosters its healthy development;

— to fight for the total abolition of the leasing system as a system of land tenancy and for the conversion of all tenants and occupants into proprietors of the land they work.

Another example of the way in which a peasant organisation expresses the peasants' frustration with their present situation and their demand for reform appeared in a report of a rural workers' organisation in another part of the world, which states that the "traditional approach to rural development has mainly centred on seeking to involve the whole community by covering all sections—the rural privileged as well as the lower-income groups—through governmental machinery, rather than being concerned with the development of voluntary, independent, free and self-reliant organisations of the rural poor for effective participation in development".

The most salient feature of the present rural scene, this organisation claimed, is the existence of a small élite which owns the greater part of the economic assets in the area and consequently corners the fruits of any development in the form of enhanced capital value; this élite exercises all the functions of social and economic leadership, dominates the channels of communication and the dissemination of information and uses its influence and "other well known methods" to control the agencies of local government and administration.

This state of affairs led the organisation to state bluntly: "It is evident that against such a well entrenched system of privilege and exploitation, no isolated individual effort can hope to prevail. The only way is collective action undertaken by an organised group of the underprivileged." Among the more important matters which required action to improve the lot of its members, the organisation listed: the reform of agrarian tenancy rights; minimum wages for agricultural workers; the availability of inputs and credits; and the removal of exploitation by money-lenders.

Activities of peasant organisations to obtain reform

Earlier, in discussing rural wage earners' organisations, we defined "pressure-group activities" as another way of saying that members' interests are presented by their organisation to government, to political parties and to society as a whole. A self-employed rural workers' organisation acts in the same way on behalf of its peasant members, and since reform is the goal of the peasants, it does so more intensively. A peasant organisation spends a far greater percentage of its income on pressure-group activities than does a rural wage earners' organisation, and a far greater percentage of the time and effort of the peasant leadership is devoted to this type of activity. As the goal is reform, it is vital that the rural workers' organisation speaking on behalf of the peasants be seen by all classes and groups in society and by political parties and government to be the voice of the peasants—the true representative of the peasants.

Thus once again, organising potential members is the first step in pressure-group activities: as many peasants as possible in each category and in each region of the country must be encouraged to join and become dues-paying members of the organisation.

With regard to relations with political parties, peasant organisations have the same variety of relationships as do the rural wage earners' organisations discussed earlier; but again, because of the interest of their members in agrarian reform, peasant organisations are generally more active in this sphere than are organisations of rural wage earners, whatever may be the nature of their relationship to political parties.

Those peasant organisations which have no relationship with any party are militant in their support of candidates, of whatever party, who have publicly demonstrated their support for the reforms that the peasant seeks. More peasant organisations than rural wage earners' organisations permit their officials to become candidates for election to legislatures or parliaments; indeed, the election of peasants and their chosen representatives to all levels of government is generally looked upon as a means of increasing the pressure for reform.

Peasant organisations cannot take strike action as a means of applying pressure in the same way as rural wage earners can; but they can and do apply pressure in similar ways. Peasant organisations promote mass rallies and demonstrations in provincial and national capitals on appropriate national holidays or when reform laws are under consideration, as a means of "voting with their feet", of standing up where parties, government and society can count them, of showing their solidarity and of expressing their need for reform.

In order to alert public opinion to the economic, social and political problems of the peasants, some peasant organisations have resorted to planned, disciplined occupations of land in a selected area and situation.

In all developing countries where the peasants' need is for economic, social and political reform, their organisations aim at obtaining mass support from as many groups as possible. As one peasant organisation has said: "Organisations must also be capable of exercising responsible pressure for furthering and protecting the interests of their members. Responsible pressure is representation on behalf of the members to secure legislative or executive action directly impacting on the well-being of the rural lower-income groups, and the seeking of large-scale group or even mass support in obtaining their objectives."

To inform the various groups and society as a whole of the peasants' need for reform, and to gain their support, peasant organisations spend as much of their resources as possible on obtaining publicity through newspapers and radio and television programmes; some even run their own newspapers and radio programmes for this purpose.

Participation of peasant organisations as part of reform

Rural wage earners seek representation on bodies which define policy and which administer the legislation and policy that affect their interests. Peasants, however, whilst accepting that agrarian reform may be an essential element in national economic development, seek above all economic and social justice for themselves. They therefore seek not only representation but also participation—and they want that participation to be a part of the reform. If agrarian reform is left solely to economists, sociologists, agricultural technicians and politicians, as far as the peasants are concerned this amounts to no real change, no reform—because for generations past others have been controlling them and directing them whilst claiming to look after their interests.

Because the peasants cannot wait until they and their organisations have enough strength or influence to secure a place on all the bodies, committees and institutes that are part of the policy-making and administrative apparatus of agrarian reform, they demand, as a basic element of agrarian reform, that from the outset the peasants and their chosen representatives be accepted as part of that apparatus.

In some developing countries where agrarian reform has been instituted by decree or legislation, the peasants and their organisations have participated in its formulation and in its implementation. There are also a number of instances where the principal officials of peasant organisations are by law officials of national councils on agrarian reform, national agrarian reform institutes, the management board of national agricultural banks, national co-ordinating economic councils, planning boards within ministries of agriculture, agricultural extension service boards, rural housing boards, national institutes of education, commodity boards within ministries of agriculture, national credit boards, and committees for the settlement of state lands.[1]

These examples at the national level are duplicated and multiplied at the regional, provincial and local levels. Indeed, in some developing countries where because of inadequate government revenue the institution of effective local government in rural areas has not been possible, base or local units of peasant organisations, through community development programmes, often perform many of the functions of a local government body by themselves

---

[1] See again the sections of Convention No. 141 and Recommendation No. 149 referred to on p. 101.

providing local roads, water systems, schools and medical dispensaries. In situations where land reform provides for settlement on previously unoccupied or virgin lands, the executive committee of the base or local unit of the peasant organisation may even become the *de facto* local government.

Questions and points for discussion

1. What are the most important immediate needs of the peasants in your country? Is agrarian reform important to them? What kind(s) of reform do they seek? Is their organisation represented on the bodies concerned with the implementation of an existing agrarian reform programme?

2. If there is a peasant organisation in your country, what are the main issues it raises on behalf of its members through pressure-group activities? How successful is it in attaining its objectives? Has it the strength of membership necessary really to influence public and government opinion?

3. If there is no peasant organisation in your country, what are the issues which you feel a newly created organisation would have to tackle? What can you personally do to help in the formation of such an organisation?

Other services for self-employed rural workers

14

Whilst agrarian reform is the main preoccupation of most peasant organisations, the reforms they seek do not come about overnight. In the meantime members have many needs which the organisation can further and defend—indeed, it is essential for it to do so if it is to stay alive. No group of workers will continue to pay contributions to an organisation indefinitely, simply in the hope of reform. They need to see some practical returns for their money. Even when reforms have been set in motion, the peasant organisation can perform many services for its members in addition to those directly concerned with the reform itself. Here we review some of the ways in which peasant organisations can and do tackle these issues.

Legal services

On a day-to-day basis, some of the most important needs of peasants are of a legal or legal-administrative nature. Many strong national peasant organisations handle a thousand or more of such individual cases each year through their legal services. Among the major problems encountered are: evictions of sharecroppers or tenants; violations of laws on sharecropping or tenancy, where these exist; disputes over crop sharing; disputes over title to land; and disputes over minimum wages and similar matters of concern to wage earners (for many self-employed rural workers also become temporary wage earners when they have the opportunity). New laws or decrees generate a considerable need for immediate service: for example, when a law is passed or a decree issued stating that anyone who has worked a plot of land for 5, 10 or 20 years (as the case may be) is now the proprietor of that plot of land, a tremendous, immediate effort by the peasant organisation in providing a legal and legal-administrative service to its members is called for. The legal expertise available to the organisation is needed to analyse all aspects of the law or decree, to determine how claims must be processed and filed so as to be legal and binding, to determine how long the

107

processing will take and to estimate the costs of such processing. On the basis of these technical considerations, the whole executive, administrative and field forces of the organisation will have to be mobilised to send specific detailed information to all base units and thus to all members of the organisation, to send the appropriate forms to all eligible members, to bring the forms back and to have them duly processed by the appropriate authorities.

Many of the legal and legal-administrative services of peasant organisations are, of course, less dramatic; but these examples serve to emphasise that legal services are very important to peasants and that an organisation must be prepared to provide such services to meet emergency situations— whether the emergency is positive (as in the example above) or negative.

Information and educational activities

We have seen that from the start rural wage earners' organisations pay considerable attention to supplementing the "organisational" methods of making information available to members by such means as newsletters and newspapers, and also to the trade union education of members and of potential officers and officials. If anything, the emphasis on these activities is even greater in peasant organisations. Generally, the peasant is likely to have less knowledge and experience than the wage earner of trade unionism and of the organisation of workers for furthering and defending their interests.

The communications systems developed by peasant organisations range from an informal, personal "passing the word" (an activity in which the field representatives and local officers have a vital role to play) to information bulletins, newspapers and even "spots" on radio programmes or union-run radio programmes. The subjects which may be covered range from matters of internal organisation and views on policy and legal matters affecting members' interests to agrarian and other types of information which can assist members to maintain or increase production on their land and to obtain the best cash return for their labour. In peasant organisations it is even more important than in wage earners' organisations that information does not flow one way only (see figure 2). The administration has to ensure that there are adequate channels through which it can be constantly and fully informed of the views, aspirations and reactions of the members.

Furthermore, since peasant organisations consider their participation in the organs of agrarian reform to be part of the reform, they have had to educate peasants in a wide variety of subjects not previously thought of as being relevant to trade union or workers' education. There are examples of peasant organisations introducing courses on the development of agrarian reform, including ways of working more effectively at the various levels with, or as a part of, such governmental bodies as agrarian institutes, ministries and banks. General trade union and workers' education courses conducted by peasant organisations, particularly those for officers and officials, often include such subjects as the principles of agrarian reform, the use of agricultural credits, the management of agricultural commodities, community development and the principles of co-operative activities.[1]

Special services to meet members' needs [2]

Peasant organisations are well aware of the special needs of their members. Many of these needs are the same as those of rural wage earners, discussed earlier: unemployment and underemployment, illiteracy, special needs of youth and of women, consumer needs, credit needs, health care needs, and so on. Peasant organisations at the national level insist that many of these special needs are a part of the agrarian problem as a whole and that they must therefore be dealt with by demanding and applying pressure for agrarian reform.

There are nevertheless many examples of peasant organisations providing services direct to their members. For example, some are directly sponsoring literacy campaigns and programmes, either alone or jointly with governments and institutes, and some are sponsoring similar projects for women on such subjects as nutrition, health care, family care and family planning.

The two main categories of service developed by peasant organisations to meet the special needs of members are, however, co-operatives or co-operative-type schemes and community development.

Co-operative-type schemes [3]

Depending on the national laws relating to co-operatives and unions, and on the type of activity undertaken, many peasant organisations are developing either union co-operatives or co-operative-type enterprises or schemes as a service to their members. The relationships between peasant organisations and peasant co-operatives are diverse and complex. For instance, some peasant federations have local agricultural co-operatives of rural workers among their affiliated base units. In other cases the peasants have found that a trade-union-type peasant organisation cannot, under the law in force, obtain legal recognition and they have used the co-operative laws as a means of obtaining legal status. Once a peasant organisation is established, it frequently happens that certain particular interests of the members are best served through a co-operative or through a co-operative-type activity. Once this stage has been reached, a further variety of forms may develop:

— the peasant organisation may decide that a separate co-operative is not necessary; the existing organisational structure and personnel is then used to provide the same service as a co-operative;

---

[1] See footnote to p. 89 for further information on workers' education methods and techniques for rural workers and their organisations.

[2] See footnote to p. 90 concerning special services.

[3] See footnote to p. 93 concerning co-operative principles.

— the peasant organisation may decide that a separate co-operative would be the best means of providing a particular service to members, but may then find that the laws on co-operatives do not allow it to confine the service to the members of the organisation. It may then decide either to establish a co-operative which would make its services available to all (in which case it may not be able to retain control of the service and the value of the service to the organisation may be lessened, because non-members would benefit from it without having to support the other work of the organisation), or to operate the service within the organisation without establishing a separate formal co-operative; or

— the peasant organisation may find that it can establish a separate co-operative and still confine its service to members of the organisation. In this case (since the control of the co-operative is in the hands of its members, who are also members of the organisation) the policy and the service remain under the control of the organisation.

However, whatever the reason for the co-operative or co-operative-type activity and whatever form it may take, all such activities are a means to a common end: to provide a special service required by members of the peasant organisation. Several strong national peasant organisations and unified rural workers' organisations (peasants and wage earners) have established and developed such schemes for the following purposes: to engage in the purchase and distribution of fertilisers and agricultural chemicals and machinery; to establish and operate primary processing mills; to extend crop loans; to set up irrigation systems; and to conduct courses relating to services provided by the organisation. Under one scheme simple agricultural machinery has been imported direct, serviced and repaired; as a result the prices to members are 20 to 30 per cent lower than market prices. Under another scheme the produce of member base units is taken to nearby large cities for sale to urban consumer co-operatives; the unreasonable charges of the middle men are thereby bypassed, with the result that members receive higher prices for their produce whilst at the same time the prices to urban consumers are lowered.

When members obtain land through agrarian reform, some national rural workers' organisations assist them, on request, with technical advice on setting up producer and marketing co-operatives.

Community development

Community development projects make as much use as possible of the donated labour of the local population, together with voluntary assessments in cash based on ability to pay.

Many of these projects originate and take place at the base or local units of peasant organisations. While some community development projects are carried out without the participation of peasant organisations, many are organised by the local officers of these organisations; others are based on the local unit, and many receive guidance and technical assistance from the national peasant organisation.

The projects undertaken cover the range of activities that are normally considered to be the responsibility of local government: provision of drinking water, a road to the next town, a bridge, a medical clinic, a school house, a market, a social centre, and so on.

Some relatively new types of service for the unemployed are being undertaken at the community level by national peasant organisations, particularly in those countries where there are large numbers of landless labourers in the rural sector. Through technical assistance and loans from national and international rural workers' organisations, the local units of peasant organisations are developing schemes for raising silkworms, fish in tanks, dairy and poultry where none existed before, and for setting up weaving and other cottage-type industries.

Questions and points for discussion

1. If there is a peasant organisation in your country, which interests of its members is it seeking to further and defend through services other than pressure-group activities? Can you think of other services which it might usefully perform? Why do you think the organisation is not already performing those services?

2. If there is no peasant organisation in your country, assume that you are an official of a newly formed organisation. How would you recommend that the organisation should set about deciding on the type of non-pressure-group services it can or should provide? What financial, technical and personnel resources would be required to run such services, and how would you propose they might be secured?

Part IV

Conclusion

The rural workers' organisation as a whole 15

Our examination of the structure and functions of rural workers' organisations began with two definitions: what is meant by "rural workers" and what is meant by a "rural workers' organisation". Everything in this book is intended to widen and deepen our understanding of these two terms and to broaden our knowledge of the many methods by which the rural worker is served by his or her rural workers' organisation.

We looked first at rural workers in terms of their numbers, and found that over two-thirds of the world's population live and work in rural areas. We also found that in almost all the developing countries rural workers account for well over half the total number of workers in the country—in some they represent as much as 90 per cent of the labour force. It was noted that their conditions of life and work vary greatly around the world; and we found that some 900 million human beings are members of rural workers' families and have an annual average income of less than US$100.

We looked briefly at the background and history of rural workers' organisations around the world, observing the struggle of all workers to gain recognition of their right to organise—that is, freedom of association. We examined the development of the right of rural workers to organise as expressed in the International Labour Code, noting the very special role of the ILO in the adoption of international labour Conventions to further the recognition of the basic rights of all workers. Attention was drawn to the particular importance of the Rural Workers' Organisations Convention, 1975 (No. 141), which specifically defines the various categories of rural worker and affirms that all have the right of association. Some of the obstacles at the national and local levels to the exercise of these trade union rights by rural workers were also noted; the struggle for the full recognition of the rural workers' rights goes on.

At this point, we began to take apart the rural workers' organisations to analyse their structure—to see how they are designed to serve the interests of rural workers. We noted that there exists a wide range of structures reflecting the history and culture in which rural workers' organisations are formed. The "flesh" of these organisations—their physical features—and the "bones"—their constitutional features—were analysed. We found that these organisations are formed according to categories of rural worker—some are peasant organisations, some wage earners' organisations, some mixed membership organisations. We looked at the local or base unit of these organisations and at its importance as the first point of contact between the rural worker and his or her union. We examined the regional or occupational committees, the supreme authority (delegate assembly) and the constitutional leadership. Some organisations serve the rural workers in one area or enterprise; others are national in scope. Some have a "centralised" administration and policy; in others, the local units are loosely affiliated to a co-ordinating federation.

We examined the "nerves and muscles"—the administrative features— of rural workers' organisations: administration at the local unit and at the national level; the need for every member to be an activist; the important role of field representatives; the need for effective two-way communication within an organisation; the necessity of maintaining and extending membership; and, above all, the provision of services to members.

We analysed in some detail the "life's blood"—the financial features— of rural workers' organisations. We looked closely at the organisations' need for finances; at the nature of the financial contributions of members; at the ability of even the poorest rural workers to pay; at methods of collection of dues; at principles and practices related to the distribution of dues within the organisation; and at external sources of finances and problems related to these. We had the opportunity to examine the record-keeping and reporting functions as they relate to a rural workers' organisation.

Finally, we examined in some detail the tremendous variety of interests of the various categories of rural worker and we took special care to observe how a rural workers' organisation goes about furthering and defending these interests: representation by collective bargaining; representation by pressure-group activities; participation in agrarian reform; participation in the formation of national policy and legislation; representation in national and local administration; legal services; union benefits; information and educational activities; and services developed to meet the special needs of members.

We took the rural workers' organisation apart to analyse it; but it is important that we realise that, while each aspect we have considered is important, even vital, it is nevertheless but a part of the whole—and it is only the whole which can be effective.

Whether we are involved in starting a new organisation, participating in the development of a young organisation or evaluating and seeking ways of making more effective an older organisation, we must be certain that all the "parts" are present and in some degree of balance. There is no way in which an organisation can effectively further and defend the interests of the rural poor with one or more of its parts missing or poorly developed. For example, a democratic constitutional structure and centralised policy will accomplish little if there is no effective administrative structure to carry out the decisions of the membership. Again, a local or enterprise union may have all its parts well developed, only to realise that many of the most important interests of its members can be successfully furthered and defended only at the national level.

A delegate assembly or executive committee may draw up a beautifully phrased manifesto on the injustices being suffered by the members and on the reforms demanded; but without financial resources from members' dues to carry out the necessary pressure-group activities, it will remain but poetry; and the lack of practical improvements can only result in the disillusionment of the peasants towards rural workers' organisations. A wage earners' organisation may have the strength and numbers to negotiate successfully with the employers, only to find that the members are dissatisfied with the agreement reached—showing a lack of two-way communication between the members and the leaders, the leaders and the members.

All the structures and functions examined are related to each other; only by giving constant attention to each and all can the organisation be made and kept strong. Ultimately, the most important interest of a rural worker is his union; for without that union, the rural worker is back to furthering and defending his interests with "the feeble strength of one".

Appendices

Guidelines for the management of finances

A

This appendix is intended for those who may have special responsibility for the handling, recording or management of an organisation's finances.

Central accounts and records

In order to function effectively, there are several items of information that every organisation needs to have about its finances. It must know the exact amount of its income and what its expenses are. At any time, it should be able to determine how much "cash in hand" and "cash in bank" it has. From this information an organisation is able to determine whether or not it is functioning well and if its money is being used in the best interests of the members.

Accounting records

The main accounting record that can give the leaders of the organisation this information is the cash book. Every organisation should open a cash book that will readily provide an analysis of receipts and payments to assist in the preparation of monthly financial reports.

A typical page of a cash book is reproduced in figure 7. The cash book system not only *records* income and expenditure; at the same time it also *analyses* both. In order to use this system the organisation must purchase a blank "analysis book", making sure that it has sufficient columns for the organisation's needs.

Let us see how the cash book operates. All moneys received are entered on the left-hand side of the book and all payments made are entered on the right-hand side: there are entry columns for "cash" and "bank" on each side of the book. In order to avoid confusion, the two cash columns and the two bank columns should be regarded as separate accounts.

The first entry on the "receipts" (left-hand) side of the cash book is the

Figure 7. Specimen page of a cash book

Receipts						Payments										
Date	Description	Receipt No.	Cash	Bank	Members' dues	Other	Date	Description	Cheque No.	P.V. No.[1]	Cash	Bank	Salaries	Transport	Post and telephone	Rent, water, etc.	Education and services	Other

[1] *P.V. No. = Payment voucher number.*

amount or balance "brought forward" from the previous page. After that, any money received will be entered on the left-hand side of the cash book in the column marked "cash", with a corresponding entry made in the appropriate receipts columns (dues or other receipts) to indicate the source of the cash received.

Any cash payments out of the funds will be entered in the column marked "cash" on the "payments" (right-hand) side of the cash book, with a corresponding entry made in the appropriate payments columns. The same operation is performed if a payment is made by cheque, except that the amount in entered in the "bank" column.

All moneys received must be deposited in the organisation's bank account. Under no circumstances should the treasurer pay expenses with cash collections before they have been banked. A payment voucher (see figure 8) should be prepared for each expenditure item and each voucher should be signed by the proper officer or official, as required by the organisation's rules. These vouchers should be numbered and filed in a folder in the order received.

Sometimes an organisation will find it necessary to withdraw money from its bank account to make a payment in cash. Such a withdrawal is not an expenditure item; the union is merely receiving its money back from the bank for safe keeping in the office until it is used for payment. The treasurer, together with other authorised signatories, will draw a cheque marked "cash" for the exact amount required. The treasurer will then make an entry on the "payments" side in the "bank" column for the amount of the cheque; but since the money will be paid into his "cash in hand" he must make an entry for a similar amount in the "cash" column on the "receipts" side of the cash book. This is called a "contrary" or "contra" entry. It is advisable to use ink of a different colour to indicate this type of entry (bank deposits and withdrawals) as well as to write a "C" (for "contrary") on both sides of the book.

At the end of each month, the treasurer must "balance the books". This means that he must determine the balance of the "cash in hand" and "cash in bank".

To determine the "cash balance", the treasurer must add up the cash received on the left-hand or receipts side of the cash book and must deduct the total of the cash column on the right-hand or payments side. The difference will be the cash balance—and the actual cash in hand should amount to the same figure.

To determine the "bank balance", the treasurer must add up the receipts in the bank column on the left-hand side of the cash book and deduct the total payments in the bank column on the right-hand side of the cash book. The difference will be the bank balance. This balance may not agree with the bank statement if deposits in the bank have not yet been credited on the statement, and/or if cheques have not yet been debited to the organisation's account (see "How to reconcile a bank statement" below).

Figure 8. Specimen payment voucher

Name of organisation   Amount _____

Paid to _____

_____

the amount of _____

_____

in respect of _____

_____

Signature of   Signature of
responsible officer   recipient   Date

_____   _____   _____

The treasurer must add up the remaining columns on both sides of the cash book. On the receipts side, the total of the remaining columns should equal the total of the cash and bank columns (less any "contrary" entries). On the payments side, the combined total of the remaining columns should also equal the total of the cash and bank columns (less any "contrary" entries). If there are discrepancies they must be due to a mistake either in making the entries or in adding up the figures. Those mistakes have to be found, accounted for and corrected. When this step is completed and no discrepancies and/or differences are noted, the cash and bank balances will be entered on the left-hand side of the following page as "balance brought forward".

How to reconcile a bank statement

1. When the bank statement is received from the bank, compare the cheque-book with the statement to verify that all cheques charged against the account are correct and that there are no entries on the statement for which there are no cheques.

2. Check the deposit book with the deposits as shown on the statement to see that the organisation has received credit for all deposits, and that only the organisation's deposits are shown on the statement. Report any discrepancies to the bank immediately. If any service charges made by the bank (e.g. for cheque-books) are shown on the statement, enter them on the payments side of the cash book.

3. If all entries on the bank statement are correct, make a list of cheques which have been issued but which are not yet listed on the bank statement. List the cheque numbers and add up the amounts involved to arrive at a figure for the value of cheques still outstanding.

4. If any entries in the bank column (of the receipts side of the cash book) do not yet appear in the deposits listed by the bank, make a list of these amounts and add them up to determine the amount of deposits not credited.

5. Enter here the balance shown on the statement .. _____

6. Add deposits not yet credited .. .. _____

                                                   Total .. .. _____

7. Subtract cheques outstanding .. .. _____

8. This is the balance (which should agree with the balance in the cash book) .. .. _____

Budget preparation

To make the best possible use of the members' money in furthering and defending their interests, one must have a financial plan approved by the members. This plan is helpful to the leaders of the organisation in carrying out their duties and is called a budget (see figure 9). A budget is an estimate of income and expenditure for a given period, usually a year. Before the end of the organisation's financial year, the treasurer, assisted by the officials or officers and some union members, should prepare estimates of the next year's income and expenditure. The estimates will be based on the organisation's experience from the current year. This budget should be presented to, for instance, the executive committee (as representatives of the members). Once approved, the budget should be regarded as a guide to the officials or officers in spending the organisation's funds. They should not normally deviate from the amount which has been allotted to them for carrying out the various activities. If for some very good reason they do so, they should be prepared to explain why.

It must be remembered that a budget is only an estimate. Unexpected developments may arise, making it necessary to modify the budget. However, the very preparation of a budget denotes that intelligent planning for which all organisations are striving.

When the treasurer periodically prepares his report of receipts and payments (see below, "Financial statements"), the officers or officials can compare the actual figures with the budgeted figures to see how the finances of the union are progressing. If the expenditure on one item is too high, they can seek to remedy the situation. If the income is not as high as anticipated, they can find out the cause.

Figure 9.   Specimen income and expenditure account, based on actual figures for the year 1977 and budgeted figures for the year 1978 (in NU)

Income	1977 (actual)	1978 (budget)	Expenditure	1977 (actual)	1978 (budget)
Dues	18 000	20 000	Salaries	1 800	1 950
Other income	1 500	1 300	Transport	3 750	4 125
			Post and telephone	1 500	1 650
			Rent, water, etc.	450	495
			Education and services	2 700	3 000
			Excess of income over expenditure	9 300	10 080
TOTAL	19 500	21 300		19 500	21 300

Financial statements

The leadership of any workers' organisation must make periodic financial reports to the membership. Financial statements provide a way for the treasurer to account to the members for his handling of the organisation's funds. They also serve as a very useful guide for the union officers and officials in leading the organisation.

We have seen above how to set about the proper, systematic method of collecting and summarising the receipts and payments of the organisation. From the monthly totals of the cash book we can easily prepare the necessary financial statements of the organisation.

At the end of each month, the totals of the cash book can be transferred to a monthly summary of receipts and payments (see figure 10). This schedule enables the organisation to summarise receipts and payments over a period of one year. The yearly totals can then be used to prepare the annual statement of income and expenditure (see figure 11).

A simple balance sheet (see figure 12) must also be drawn up showing the assets (what the organisation owns) and the liabilities (what the organisation owes).

Trustees

Two or more trustees should be appointed by the members, to supervise the funds and property of the organisation. It is the trustees' duty to see that the treasurer performs his functions properly. Another important duty of the trustees is to see that an audit is performed at least once a year, either by themselves or by a professional accountant. This is the best method of assuring the members that their money is being properly handled.

Figure 10. Specimen monthly summary of receipts and payments

	Jan.	Feb.	Mar.	Apr.	May	June	July	Aug.	Sep.	Oct.	Nov.	Dec.	Total
1. Cash and bank balance, beginning of period (from cash and bank columns)													
2. *Receipts*													
(a) Dues													
(b) Other													
3. Total receipts (item 2*(a)* plus item 2*(b)*)													
4. Total receipts plus opening balance (item 1 plus item 3)													
5. *Payments*													
(a) Salaries													
(b) Transport													
(c) Post and telephone													
(d) Rent, water, etc.													
(e) Education and services													
(f) Other													
6. Total payments (total of items 5*(a)* to 5*(f)*)													
7. Cash and bank balance, end of period (subtract item 6 from item 4)													

Figure 11.   Specimen statement of income and expenditure for the year ended 31 December 1977 (in NU)

Income		Expenditure	
Dues	18 000	Salaries	1 800
Other income	1 500	Transport	3 750
		Post and telephone	1 500
		Rent, water, etc.	450
		Education and services	2 700
		Excess of income over expenditure	9 300
TOTAL	19 500		19 500

Audit procedure

By "audit" is meant the careful and systematic examination of the organisation's books and financial records, to see that they are in order. Rules regarding audit procedure will vary from one organisation to another, but the following procedure is one in general use:

1. Arrange with the treasurer to obtain all account books and records that the organisation maintains.
2. See that all columns of figures in the cash book are correctly added and that no payments have been made contrary to the organisation's rules.
3. Check the receipts side of the cash book against the receipts issued to the collectors, ascertaining in particular that all the receipts have been listed.
4. Check the payments side of the cash book against the payment vouchers, invoices and other supporting data. Discrepancies over any item of expenditure should be referred to the officials or officers of the organisation and, if not properly explained, eventually to the general membership.
5. Reconcile the bank statement (using the procedure described earlier) and determine that all receipts for the month have been deposited into the bank.
6. Check the cash in the treasurer's possession and see that it agrees with the cash balance in the cash book.
7. Examine and certify the balance sheet.

The following check-list should be filled in as the audit is carried out. Each question should be answered with an unqualified "yes" or "no". If the answer is "no", an explanatory note must be attached. For example, if a receipt is missing, the explanatory note would record the explanation given by the

*Figure 12.   Specimen balance sheet as at 31 December 1977
(in NU)*

Assets			Liabilities		
Fixed assets			Sundry creditors		
Office furniture	1 500		(as per schedule)		750
Equipment	2 250	3 750	Capital		
			(accumulated fund)	15 450	
Current assets			Add: excess income		
Sundry debtors			(from income and		
(as per schedule)		1 800	expenditure account)	9 300	24 750
Dues in arrears		3 600			
Cash in bank		15 450			
Cash in hand		750			
Petty cash		150			
		25 500			25 500

I, _____, Treasurer, solemnly declare that the above state-
ment of accounts of the organisation is true and correct to the best of my knowledge and belief.

Signature _____

Date _____

treasurer, state what has been done to obtain the missing receipt and say
whether, in the auditor's opinion, the explanation is satisfactory.

Check-list for the use of auditors

1. Are all entries written in ink? _____
2. Have all receipts been properly obtained and filed? _____
3. Have receipts been given for all moneys received? _____
4. Are the members' cards and collectors' books in order? _____
5. Do the collectors' receipts agree with the entries in the cash book? _____
6. Have all bills been paid? _____
7. Are you satisfied that all payments made are in accordance with the rules of the organisation and the decisions of the executive committee? _____
8. Have all cheques been signed in accordance with the organisa-tion's rules? _____

9. Have all columns been added up correctly? _____

10. Have all totals been carried forward correctly? _____

11. Does the cash in hand agree with the cash balance shown in the accounts? _____

12. Do the accounts agree with the bank paying-in book and statements? _____

13. Is the annual statement of receipts and payments properly drawn up? _____

The foregoing procedures are precise, and for those who are not used to figures they can be demanding. But they are critical to the success and stability of any voluntary organisation and must be faithfully carried out. If they are not carried out to the letter, trouble will be sure to follow—if for no other reason than that those responsible for the organisation's finances will get into a muddle. "Trouble" with finances is the surest way of losing members' confidence and support; without that support, and with finances that are not in order, the organisation is not in a position to further and defend the interests of its members—and that is the reason for its existence. If an organisation should wane or die because of financial trouble, it will be a long time before anyone can again organise those rural workers who were its members.

Of all the elements that go to make up the structure and functions of a rural workers' organisation, the proper recording, handling and management of the moneys entrusted to the organisation by the members is *the* most important. For this reason this appendix has no section of "Questions and points for discussion". Its contents are not open to discussion. They must be diligently and rigorously applied.

International labour standards relating to rural workers

B

Convention No. 11

Convention concerning the Rights of Association and Combination of Agricultural Workers

The General Conference of the International Labour Organisation,

Having been convened at Geneva by the Governing Body of the International Labour Office, and having met in its Third Session on 25 October 1921, and

Having decided upon the adoption of certain proposals with regard to the rights of association and combination of agricultural workers, which is included in the fourth item of the agenda of the session, and

Having determined that these proposals shall take the form of an international Convention,

adopts the following Convention, which may be cited as the Right of Association (Agriculture) Convention, 1921, for ratification by the Members of the International Labour Organisation in accordance with the provisions of the Constitution of the International Labour Organisation:

Article 1

Each Member of the International Labour Organisation which ratifies this Convention undertakes to secure to all those engaged in agriculture the same rights of association and combination as to industrial workers, and to repeal any statutory or other provisions restricting such rights in the case of those engaged in agriculture.

. . . .

Convention No. 87

Convention concerning Freedom of Association and Protection of the Right to Organise

The General Conference of the International Labour Organisation,

Having been convened at San Francisco by the Governing Body of the International Labour Office, and having met in its Thirty-first Session on 17 June 1948;

Having decided to adopt, in the form of a Convention, certain proposals concerning freedom of association and protection of the right to organise, which is the seventh item on the agenda of the session;

Considering that the Preamble to the Constitution of the International Labour Organisation declares "recognition of the principle of freedom of association" to be a means of improving conditions of labour and of establishing peace;

Considering that the Declaration of Philadelphia reaffirms that "freedom of expression and of association are essential to sustained progress";

Considering that the International Labour Conference, at its Thirtieth Session, unanimously adopted the principles which should form the basis for international regulation;

Considering that the General Assembly of the United Nations, at its Second Session, endorsed these principles and requested the International Labour Organisation to continue every effort in order that it may be possible to adopt one or several international Conventions;

adopts this ninth day of July of the year one thousand nine hundred and forty-eight the following Convention, which may be cited as the Freedom of Association and Protection of the Right to Organise Convention, 1948:

PART I. FREEDOM OF ASSOCIATION

Article 1

Each Member of the International Labour Organisation for which this Convention is in force undertakes to give effect to the following provisions.

Article 2

Workers and employers, without distinction whatsoever, shall have the right to establish and, subject only to the rules of the organisation concerned, to join organisations of their own choosing without previous authorisation.

Article 3

1. Workers' and employers' organisations shall have the right to draw up their constitutions and rules, to elect their representatives in full freedom, to organise their administration and activities and to formulate their programmes.

2. The public authorities shall refrain from any interference which would restrict this right or impede the lawful exercise thereof.

Article 4

Workers' and employers' organisations shall not be liable to be dissolved or suspended by administrative authority.

Article 5

Workers' and employers' organisations shall have the right to establish and join federations and confederations and any such organisation, federation or confederation shall have the right to affiliate with international organisations of workers and employers.

Article 6

The provisions of Articles 2, 3 and 4 hereof apply to federations and confederations of workers' and employers' organisations.

Article 7

The acquisition of legal personality by workers' and employers' organisations, federations and confederations shall not be made subject to conditions of such a character as to restrict the application of the provisions of Articles 2, 3 and 4 hereof.

Article 8

1. In exercising the rights provided for in this Convention workers and employers and their respective organisations, like other persons or organised collectivities, shall respect the law of the land.

2. The law of the land shall not be such as to impair, nor shall it be so applied as to impair, the guarantees provided for in this Convention.

Article 9

1. The extent to which the guarantees provided for in this Convention shall apply to the armed forces and the police shall be determined by national laws or regulations.

2. In accordance with the principle set forth in paragraph 8 of Article 19 of the Constitution of the International Labour Organisation the ratification of this Convention by any Member shall not be deemed to affect any existing law, award, custom or agreement in virtue of which members of the armed forces or the police enjoy any right guaranteed by this Convention.

Article 10

In this Convention the term "organisation" means any organisation of workers or of employers for furthering and defending the interests of workers or of employers.

PART II. PROTECTION OF THE RIGHT TO ORGANISE

Article 11

Each Member of the International Labour Organisation for which this Convention is in force undertakes to take all necessary and appropriate measures to ensure that workers and employers may exercise freely the right to organise.

. . . .

Convention No. 98

Convention concerning the Application of the Principles of the Right to Organise and to Bargain Collectively

The General Conference of the International Labour Organisation,

Having been convened at Geneva by the Governing Body of the International Labour Office, and having met in its Thirty-second Session on 8 June 1949, and

Having decided upon the adoption of certain proposals concerning the application of the principles of the right to organise and to bargain collectively, which is the fourth item on the agenda of the session, and

Having determined that these proposals shall take the form of an international Convention,

adopts this first day of July of the year one thousand nine hundred and forty-nine the following Convention, which may be cited as the Right to Organise and Collective Bargaining Convention, 1949:

Article 1

1. Workers shall enjoy adequate protection against acts of anti-union discrimination in respect of their employment.

2. Such protection shall apply more particularly in respect of acts calculated to—

(a) make the employment of a worker subject to the condition that he shall not join a union or shall relinquish trade union membership;

(b) cause the dismissal of or otherwise prejudice a worker by reason of union membership or because of participation in union activities outside working hours or, with the consent of the employer, within working hours.

Article 2

1. Workers' and employers' organisations shall enjoy adequate protection against any acts of interference by each other or each other's agents or members in their establishment, functioning or administration.

2. In particular, acts which are designed to promote the establishment of workers' organisations under the domination of employers or employers' organisations, or to support workers' organisations by financial or other means, with the object of placing such organisations under the control of employers or employers' organisations, shall be deemed to constitute acts of interference within the meaning of this Article.

Article 3

Machinery appropriate to national conditions shall be established, where necessary, for the purpose of ensuring respect for the right to organise as defined in the preceding Articles.

Article 4

Measures appropriate to national conditions shall be taken, where necessary, to encourage and promote the full development and utilisation of machinery for voluntary negotiation between employers or employers' organisations and workers' organisations, with a view to the regulation of terms and conditions of employment by means of collective agreements.

Article 5

1. The extent to which the guarantees provided for in this Convention shall apply to the armed forces and the police shall be determined by national laws or regulations.

2. In accordance with the principle set forth in paragraph 8 of article 19 of the Constitution of the International Labour Organisation the ratification of this Convention by any Member shall not be deemed to affect any existing law, award, custom or agreement in virtue of which members of the armed forces or the police enjoy any right guaranteed by this Convention.

Article 6

This Convention does not deal with the position of public servants engaged in the administration of the State, nor shall it be construed as prejudicing their rights or status in any way.

. . . .

Convention No. 110

Convention concerning Conditions of Employment of Plantation Workers

The General Conference of the International Labour Organisation,

Having been convened at Geneva by the Governing Body of the International Labour Office, and having met in its Forty-second Session on 4 June 1958, and

Having considered the question of conditions of employment of plantation workers, which is the fifth item on the agenda of the session, and

Having decided that, as an exceptional measure, in order to expedite the application to plantations of certain provisions of existing Conventions, pending the more general ratification of these Conventions and the application of their provisions to all persons within their scope, and to provide for the application to plantations of certain Conventions not at present applicable thereto, it is desirable to adopt an instrument for these purposes, and

Having determined that this instrument shall take the form of an international Convention,

adopts this twenty-fourth day of June of the year one thousand nine hundred and fifty-eight the following Convention, which may be cited as the Plantations Convention, 1958:

PART I. GENERAL PROVISIONS

Article 1

1. For the purpose of this Convention, the term "plantation" includes any agricultural undertaking regularly employing hired workers which is situated in the tropical or subtropical regions and which is mainly concerned with the cultivation or production for commercial purposes of coffee, tea, sugarcane, rubber, bananas, cocoa, coconuts, groundnuts, cotton, tobacco, fibres (sisal, jute and hemp), citrus, palm oil, cinchona or pineapple; it does not include family or small-scale holdings producing for local consumption and not regularly employing hired workers.

2. Each Member for which this Convention is in force may, after consultation with the most representative organisations of employers and workers concerned, where such exist, make the Convention applicable to other plantations by—

(a) adding to the list of crops referred to in paragraph 1 of this Article any one or more of the following crops: rice, chicory, cardamom, geranium and pyrethrum, or any other crop;

(b) adding to the plantations covered by paragraph 1 of this Article classes of undertakings not referred to therein which, by national law or practice, are classified as plantations;

and shall indicate the action taken in its annual reports upon the application of the Convention submitted under article 22 of the Constitution of the International Labour Organisation.

3. For the purpose of this Article the term "plantation" shall ordinarily include services carrying out the primary processing of the product or products of the plantation.

Article 2

Each Member which ratifies this Convention undertakes to apply its provisions equally to all plantation workers without distinction as to race, colour, sex, religion, political opinion, nationality, social origin, tribe or trade union membership.

Article 3

1. Each Member for which this Convention is in force—
(a) shall comply with—
    (i) Part I;
    (ii) Parts IV, IX and XI;
    (iii) at least two of Parts II, III, V, VI, VII, VIII, X, XII and XIII; and
    (iv) Part XIV;
(b) shall, if it has excluded one or more Parts from its acceptance of the obligations of the Convention, specify, in a declaration appended to its ratification, the Part or Parts so excluded.

2. Each Member which has made a declaration under paragraph 1 *(b)* of this Article shall indicate in its annual reports submitted under article 22 of the Constitution of the International Labour Organisation any progress made towards the application of the excluded Part or Parts.

3. Each Member which has ratified the Convention, but has excluded any Part or Parts thereof under the provisions of the preceding paragraphs, may subsequently notify the Director-General of the International Labour Office that it accepts the obligations of the Convention in respect of any Part or Parts so excluded; such undertakings shall be deemed to be an integral part of the ratification and to have the force of ratification as from the date of notification.

Article 4

In accordance with article 19, paragraph 8, of the Constitution of the International Labour Organisation, nothing in this Convention shall affect any law, award, custom or agreement which ensures more favourable conditions to the workers concerned than those provided for by the Convention.

PART II. ENGAGEMENT AND RECRUITMENT OF MIGRANT WORKERS

Article 5

For the purposes of this Part of this Convention the term "recruiting" includes all operations undertaken with the object of obtaining or supplying the labour of persons who do not spontaneously offer their services at the place of employment or at a public emigration or employment office or at an office conducted by an employers' organisation and supervised by the competent authority.

Article 6

The recruiting of the head of a family shall not be deemed to involve the recruiting of any member of his family.

Article 7

No person or association shall engage in professional recruiting unless the said person or association has been licensed by the competent authority and is recruiting workers for a public department or for one or more specific employers or organisations of employers.

Article 8

Employers, employers' agents, organisations of employers, organisations subsidised by employers, and the agents of organisations of employers and of organisations subsidised by employers shall only engage in recruiting if licensed by the competent authority.

Article 9

1. Recruited workers shall be brought before a public officer, who shall satisfy himself that the law and regulations concerning recruiting have been observed and, in particular, that the workers have not been subjected to illegal pressure or recruited by misrepresentation or mistake.

2. Recruited workers shall be brought before such an officer as near as may be convenient to the place of recruiting or, in the case of workers recruited in one territory for employment in a territory under a different administration, at latest at the place of departure from the territory of recruiting.

Article 10

Where the circumstances make the adoption of such a provision practicable and necessary, the competent authority shall require the issue to each recruited worker who is not engaged at or near the place of recruiting of a document in writing such as a memorandum of information, a work book or a provisional contract containing such particulars as the authority may prescribe, as for example particulars of the identity of the workers, the prospective conditions of employment, and any advances of wages made to the workers.

Article 11

1. Every recruited worker shall be medically examined.

2. Where the worker has been recruited for employment at a distance from the place of recruiting, or has been recruited in one territory for employment in a territory under a different administration, the medical examination shall take place as near as may be convenient to the place of recruiting or, in the case of workers recruited in one territory for employment in a territory under a different administration, at latest at the place of departure from the territory of recruiting.

3. The competent authority may empower public officers before whom workers are brought in pursuance of Article 9 to authorise the departure prior to medical examination of workers in whose case they are satisfied—

(a) that it was and is impossible for the medical examination to take place near to the place of recruiting or at the place of departure;

(b) that the worker is fit for the journey and the prospective employment; and

(c) that the worker will be medically examined on arrival at the place of employment or as soon as possible thereafter.

4. The competent authority may, particularly when the journey of the recruited workers is of such duration and takes place under such conditions that the health of the workers is likely to be affected, require recruited workers to be examined both before departure and after arrival at the place of employment.

5. The competent authority shall ensure that all necessary measures are taken for the acclimatisation and adaptation of recruited workers and for their immunisation against disease.

Article 12

1. The recruiter or employer shall whenever possible provide transport to the place of employment for recruited workers.

2. The competent authority shall take all necessary measures to ensure—

(a) that the vehicles or vessels used for the transport of workers are suitable for such transport, are in good sanitary condition and are not overcrowded;

(b) that when it is necessary to break the journey for the night suitable accommodation is provided for the workers; and

(c) that in the case of long journeys all necessary arrangements are made for medical assistance and for the welfare of the workers.

3. When recruited workers have to make long journeys on foot to the place of employment the competent authority shall take all necessary measures to ensure—

(a) that the length of the daily journey is compatible with the maintenance of the health and strength of the workers; and

(b) that, where the extent of the movement of labour makes this necessary, rest camps or rest houses are provided at suitable points on main routes and are kept in proper sanitary condition and have the necessary facilities for medical attention.

4. When recruited workers have to make long journeys in groups to the place of employment, they shall be convoyed by a responsible person.

Article 13

1. The expenses of the journey of recruited workers to the place of employment, including all expenses incurred for their protection during the journey, shall be borne by the recruiter or employer.

2. The recruiter or employer shall furnish recruited workers with everything necessary for their welfare during the journey to the place of employment, including particularly, as local circumstances may require, adequate and suitable supplies of food, drinking water, fuel and cooking utensils, clothing and blankets.

Article 14

Any recruited worker who—

(a) becomes incapacitated by sickness or accident during the journey to the place of employment,

(b) is found on medical examination to be unfit for employment,

(c) is not engaged after recruiting for a reason for which he is not responsible, or

(d) is found by the competent authority to have been recruited by misrepresentation or mistake,

shall be repatriated at the expense of the recruiter or employer.

Article 15

Where the families of recruited workers have been authorised to accompany the workers to the place of employment the competent authority shall take all necessary measures for safeguarding their health and welfare during the journey and more particularly—

(a) Articles 12 and 13 of this Convention shall apply to such families;

(b) in the event of the worker being repatriated in virtue of Article 14, his family shall also be repatriated; and

(c) in the event of the death of the worker during the journey to the place of employment, his family shall be repatriated.

Article 16

The competent authority shall limit the amount which may be paid to recruited workers in respect of advances of wages and shall regulate the conditions under which such advances may be made.

Article 17

1. Each Member for which this Part of this Convention is in force undertakes that it will, so far as national laws and regulations permit, take all appropriate steps against misleading propaganda relating to emigration and immigration.

2. For this purpose it will, where appropriate, act in co-operation with other Members concerned.

Article 18

Measures shall be taken as appropriate by each Member, within its jurisdiction, to facilitate the departure, journey and reception of migrants for employment on a plantation.

Article 19

Each Member for which this Part of this Convention is in force undertakes to maintain, within its jurisdiction, appropriate medical services responsible for—

(a) ascertaining, where necessary, both at the time of departure and on arrival, that migrants for employment on a plantation and the members of their families authorised to accompany or join them are in reasonable health;

(b) ensuring that migrants for employment on a plantation and members of their families enjoy adequate medical attention and good hygienic conditions at the time of departure, during the journey and on arrival in the territory of destination.

PART III. CONTRACTS OF EMPLOYMENT AND ABOLITION OF PENAL SANCTIONS

Article 20

1. The law and/or regulations in force in the territory concerned shall prescribe the maximum period of service which may be stipulated or implied in any contract, whether written or oral.

2. The maximum period of service which may be stipulated or implied in any contract for employment not involving a long and expensive journey shall in no case exceed 12 months if the workers are not accompanied by their families or two years if the workers are accompanied by their families.

3. The maximum period of service which may be stipulated or implied in any contract for employment involving a long and expensive journey shall in no case exceed two years if the workers are not accompanied by their families or three years if the workers are accompanied by their families.

4. The competent authority may, after consultation with the employers' and workers' organisations representative of the interests concerned, where such exist, exclude from the application of this Part of this Convention contracts entered into between employers and non-manual workers whose freedom of choice in employment is satisfactorily safeguarded; such exclusion may apply to all plantation workers in a territory, to plantation workers engaged in the production of a particular crop, to the workers in any specified undertaking or to special groups of plantation workers.

Article 21

The competent authority in each country where there exists any penal sanction for any breach of a contract of employment by a plantation worker shall take action for the abolition of all such penal sanctions.

Article 22

Such action shall provide for the abolition of all such penal sanctions by means of an appropriate measure of immediate application.

Article 23

For the purpose of this Part of the Convention the term "breach of contract" means—

(a) any refusal or failure of the worker to commence or perform the service stipulated in the contract;

(b) any neglect of duty or lack of diligence on the part of the worker;

(c) the absence of the worker without permission or valid reason; and

(d) the desertion of the worker.

PART IV. WAGES

Article 24

1. The fixing of minimum wages by collective agreements freely negotiated between trade unions which are representative of the workers concerned and employers or employers' organisations shall be encouraged.

2. Where no adequate arrangements exist for the fixing of minimum wages by collective agreement, the necessary arrangements shall be made whereby minimum rates of wages can be fixed, where appropriate by means of national laws or regulations, in consultation with representatives of the employers and workers, including representatives of their respective organisations, where such exist, such consultation to be on a basis of complete equality.

3. Minimum rates of wages which have been fixed in accordance with arrangements made in pursuance of the preceding paragraph shall be binding on the employers and workers concerned so as not to be subject to abatement.

Article 25

1. Each Member for which this Convention is in force shall take the necessary measures to ensure that the employers and workers concerned are informed of the minimum rates of wages in force and that wages are not paid at less than these rates in cases where they are applicable; these measures shall include such provision for supervision, inspection, and sanction as may be necessary and appropriate to the conditions obtaining on plantations in the country concerned.

2. A worker to whom the minimum rates are applicable and who has been paid wages at less than these rates shall be entitled to recover, by judicial or other appropriate proceedings, the amount by which he has been underpaid, subject to such limitations of time as may be determined by national laws or regulations.

Article 26

Wages payable in money shall be paid only in legal tender, and payment in the form of promissory notes, vouchers or coupons, or in any other form alleged to represent legal tender, shall be prohibited.

Article 27

1. National laws or regulations, collective agreements or arbitration awards may authorise the partial payment of wages in the form of allowances in kind where payment in the form of such allowances is customary or desirable; the payment of

wages in the form of liquor of high alcoholic content or of noxious drugs shall not be permitted in any circumstances.

2. In cases in which partial payment of wages in the form of allowances in kind is authorised, appropriate measures shall be taken to ensure that such allowances are appropriate for the personal use and benefit of the worker and his family.

3. Where food, housing, clothing and other essential supplies and services form part of remuneration, all practicable steps shall be taken to ensure that they are adequate and their cash value properly assessed.

Article 28

Wages shall be paid directly to the worker concerned except as may be otherwise provided by national laws or regulations, collective agreement or arbitration award or where the worker concerned has agreed to the contrary.

Article 29

Employers shall be prohibited from limiting in any manner the freedom of the worker to dispose of his wages.

Article 30

1. Where works stores for the sale of commodities to the workers are established or services are operated in connection with an undertaking, the workers concerned shall be free from any coercion to make use of such stores or services.

2. Where access to other stores or services is not possible, the competent authority shall take appropriate measures with the object of ensuring that goods are sold and services provided at fair and reasonable prices, or that stores established and services operated by the employer are not operated for the purpose of securing a profit but for the benefit of the workers concerned.

Article 31

1. Deductions from wages shall be permitted only under conditions and to the extent prescribed by national laws or regulations or fixed by collective agreement or arbitration award.

2. Workers shall be informed, in the manner deemed most appropriate by the competent authority, of the conditions under which and the extent to which such deductions may be made.

Article 32

Any deduction from wages with a view to ensuring a direct or indirect payment for the purpose of obtaining or retaining employment, made by a worker to an employer or his representative or to any intermediary (such as a labour contractor or recruiter), shall be prohibited.

Article 33

1. Wages shall be paid regularly. Except where other appropriate arrangements exist which ensure the payment of wages at regular intervals, the intervals for the payment of wages shall be prescribed by national laws or regulations or fixed by collective agreement or arbitration award.

2. Upon the termination of a contract of employment, a final settlement of all wages due shall be effected in accordance with national laws or regulations, collective agreement or arbitration award or, in the absence of any applicable law, regulation, agreement or award, within a reasonable period of time having regard to the terms of the contract.

Article 34

Where necessary, effective measures shall be taken to ensure that workers are informed, in an appropriate and easily understandable manner—

(a) before they enter employment and when any changes take place, of the conditions in respect of wages under which they are employed; and

(b) at the time of each payment of wages, of the particulars of their wages for the pay period concerned, in so far as such particulars may be subject to change.

Article 35

The laws or regulations giving effect to the provisions of Articles 26 to 34 of this Convention shall—

(a) be made available for the information of persons concerned;

(b) define the persons responsible for compliance therewith;

(c) prescribe adequate penalties or other appropriate remedies for any violation thereof;

(d) provide for the maintenance, in all appropriate cases, of adequate records in an approved form and manner.

PART V. ANNUAL HOLIDAYS WITH PAY

Article 36

Workers employed on plantations shall be granted an annual holiday with pay after a period of continuous service with the same employer.

Article 37

1. Each Member for which this Part of this Convention is in force shall be free to decide the manner in which provision shall be made for holidays with pay on plantations.

2. Such provision may be made, where appropriate, by means of collective agreement or by entrusting the regulation of holidays with pay on plantations to special bodies.

3. Wherever the manner in which provision is made for holidays with pay on plantations permits—

(a) there shall be full preliminary consultation with the most representative organisations of employers and workers concerned, where such exist, and with any other persons, specially qualified by their trade or functions, whom the competent authority deems it useful to consult;

(b) the employers and workers concerned shall participate in the regulation of holidays with pay, or be consulted or have the right to be heard, in such manner and to such extent as may be determined by national laws or regulations, but in any case on a basis of complete equality.

Article 38

The required minimum period of continuous service and the minimum duration of the annual holiday with pay shall be determined by national laws or regulations, collective agreement or arbitration award, or by special bodies entrusted with the regulation of holidays with pay on plantations, or in any other manner approved by the competent authority.

Article 39

Where appropriate, provision shall be made, in accordance with the established procedure for the regulation of holidays with pay on plantations, for—

(a) more favourable treatment for young workers, in cases in which the annual holiday with pay granted to adult workers is not considered adequate for young workers;

(b) an increase in the duration of the annual paid holiday with the length of service;

(c) proportionate holidays or payment in lieu thereof, in cases where the period of continuous service of a worker is not of sufficient duration to qualify him for an annual holiday with pay but exceeds such minimum period as may be determined in accordance with the established procedure;

(d) the exclusion from the annual holiday with pay of public and customary holidays and weekly rest periods, and, to such extent as may be determined in accordance with the established procedure, temporary interruptions of attendance at work due to such causes as sickness or accident.

Article 40

1. Every person taking a holiday in virtue of this Part of this Convention shall receive, in respect of the full period of the holiday, not less than his usual remuneration, or such remuneration as may be prescribed in accordance with paragraphs 2 and 3 of this Article.

2. The remuneration payable in respect of the holiday shall be calculated as prescribed by national laws or regulations, collective agreement or arbitration award, or by special bodies entrusted with the regulation of holidays with pay on plantations, or in any other manner approved by the competent authority.

3. Where the remuneration of the person taking a holiday includes payments in kind, provision may be made for the payment in respect of holidays of the cash equivalent of such payments in kind.

Article 41

Any agreement to relinquish the right to an annual holiday with pay, or to forgo such a holiday, shall be void.

Article 42

A person who is dismissed or who has relinquished his employment before he has taken the whole or any part of the holiday due to him shall receive in respect of every day of holiday due to him in virtue of this Part of this Convention the remuneration provided for in Article 40.

PART VI. WEEKLY REST

Article 43

1. Plantation workers shall, except as otherwise provided for by the following Articles, enjoy in every period of seven days a period of rest comprising at least 24 consecutive hours.

2. This period of rest shall, wherever possible, be granted simultaneously to all the workers of each plantation.

3. It shall, wherever possible, be fixed so as to coincide with the days already established by the traditions or customs of the country or district.

Article 44

1. Each Member may authorise total or partial exceptions (including suspensions or diminutions) from the provisions of Article 43, special regard being had to all proper humanitarian and economic considerations and after consultation with responsible associations of employers and workers, wherever such exist.

2. Such consultation shall not be necessary in the case of exceptions which have already been made under existing legislation.

Article 45

Each Member shall make, as far as possible, provision for compensatory periods of rest for the suspensions or diminutions made in virtue of Article 44, except in cases where agreements or customs already provide for such periods.

PART VII.   MATERNITY PROTECTION

Article 46

For the purpose of this Part of this Convention, the term "woman" means any female person, irrespective of age, nationality, race or creed, whether married or unmarried, and the term "child" means any child whether born of marriage or not.

Article 47

1. A woman to whom this Part of this Convention applies shall, on the production of appropriate evidence of the presumed date of her confinement, be entitled to a period of maternity leave.

2. The competent authority may, after consultation with the most representative organisations of employers and workers, where such exist, prescribe a qualifying period for maternity leave which shall not exceed a total of 150 days of employment with the same employer during the 12 months preceding the confinement.

3. The period of maternity leave shall be at least 12 weeks, and shall include a period of compulsory leave after confinement.

4. The period of compulsory leave after confinement shall be prescribed by national laws or regulations, but shall in no case be less than six weeks; the remainder of the total period of maternity leave may be provided before the presumed date of confinement or following expiration of the compulsory leave period or partly before the presumed date of confinement and partly following the expiration of the compulsory leave period as may be prescribed by national laws or regulations.

5. The leave before the presumed date of confinement shall be extended by any period elapsing between the presumed date of confinement and the actual date of confinement, and the period of compulsory leave to be taken after confinement shall not be reduced on that account.

6. In case of illness suitably certified as arising out of pregnancy national laws or regulations shall provide for additional leave before confinement, the maximum duration of which may be fixed by the competent authority.

7. In case of illness suitably certified as arising out of confinement the woman shall be entitled to an extension of the leave after confinement, the maximum duration of which may be fixed by the competent authority.

8. No pregnant woman shall be required to undertake any type of work harmful to her in the period prior to her maternity leave.

Article 48

1. While absent from work on maternity leave in accordance with the provisions of Article 47, the woman shall be entitled to receive cash and medical benefits.

2. The rates of cash benefit shall be fixed by national laws or regulations so as to ensure benefits sufficient for the full and healthy maintenance of herself and her child in accordance with a suitable standard of living.

3. Medical benefits shall include prenatal, confinement and postnatal care by qualified midwives or medical practitioners as well as hospitalisation care where necessary; freedom of choice of doctor and freedom of choice between a public and private hospital shall be respected as far as practicable.

4. Any contribution due under a compulsory social insurance scheme providing maternity benefits and any tax based upon payrolls which is raised for the purpose of providing such benefits shall, whether paid both by the employer and the employees or by the employer, be paid in respect of the total number of men and women employed by the undertakings concerned, without distinction of sex.

Article 49

1. If a woman is nursing her child she shall be entitled to interrupt her work for this purpose, under conditions to be prescribed by national laws or regulations.

2. Interruptions of work for the purpose of nursing are to be counted as working hours and remunerated accordingly in cases in which the matter is governed by or in accordance with laws and regulations; in cases in which the matter is governed by collective agreement, the position shall be as determined by the relevant agreement.

Article 50

1. While a woman is absent from work on maternity leave in accordance with the provisions of Article 47, it shall not be lawful for her employer to give her notice of dismissal during such absence, or to give her notice of dismissal at such a time that the notice would expire during such absence.

2. The dismissal of a woman solely because she is pregnant or a nursing mother shall be prohibited.

PART VIII. WORKMEN'S COMPENSATION

Article 51

Each Member of the International Labour Organisation for which this Part of this Convention is in force undertakes to extend to all plantation workers its laws and regulations which provide for the compensation of workers for personal injury by accident arising out of or in the course of their employment.

Article 52

1. Each Member for which this Part of this Convention is in force undertakes to grant to the nationals of any other Member for which this Part of this Convention is in force, who suffer personal injury due to industrial accidents happening in its territory, or to their dependants, the same treatment in respect of workmen's compensation as it grants to its own nationals.

2. This equality of treatment shall be guaranteed to foreign workers and their dependants without any condition as to residence. With regard to the payments which a Member or its nationals would have to make outside that Member's territory in the application of this principle, the measures to be adopted shall be regulated, if necessary, by special arrangements between the Members concerned.

Article 53

Special agreements may be made between the Members concerned to provide that compensation for industrial accidents happening to workers whilst temporarily or intermittently employed in the territory of one Member on behalf of an undertaking situated in the territory of another Member shall be governed by the laws and regulations of the latter Member.

Part IX. Right to Organise and Collective Bargaining

Article 54

The right of employers and employed alike to associate for all lawful purposes shall be guaranteed by appropriate measures.

Article 55

All procedures for the investigation of disputes between employers and workers shall be as simple and expeditious as possible.

Article 56

1. Employers and workers shall be encouraged to avoid disputes and, if they arise, to reach fair settlements by means of conciliation.

2. For this purpose all practicable measures shall be taken to consult and associate the representatives of organisations of employers and workers in the establishment and working of conciliation machinery.

3. Subject to the operation of such machinery, public officers shall be responsible for the investigation of disputes and shall endeavour to promote conciliation and to assist the parties in arriving at a fair settlement.

4. Where practicable, these officers shall be officers specially assigned to such duties.

Article 57

1. Machinery shall be created as rapidly as possible for the settlement of disputes between employers and workers.

2. Representatives of the employers and workers concerned, including representatives of their respective organisations, where such exist, shall be associated where practicable in the operation of the machinery, in such manner and to such extent, but in any case in equal numbers and on equal terms, as may be determined by the competent authority.

Article 58

1. Workers shall enjoy adequate protection against acts of anti-union discrimination in respect of their employment.

2. Such protection shall apply more particularly in respect of acts calculated to—

(a) make the employment of a worker subject to the condition that he shall not join a union or shall relinquish trade union membership;

(b) cause the dismissal of or otherwise prejudice a worker by reason of union membership or because of participation in union activities outside working hours or, with the consent of the employer, within working hours.

Article 59

1. Workers' and employers' organisations shall enjoy adequate protection against any acts of interference by each other or each other's agents or members in their establishment, functioning or administration.

2. In particular, acts which are designed to promote the establishment of workers' organisations under the domination of employers or employers' organisations, or to support workers' organisations by financial or other means, with the object of placing such organisations under the control of employers or employers' organisations, shall be deemed to constitute acts of interference within the meaning of this Article.

Article 60

Machinery appropriate to national conditions shall be established, where necessary, for the purpose of ensuring respect for the right to organise as defined in the preceding Articles.

Article 61

Measures appropriate to national conditions shall be taken, where necessary, to encourage and promote the full development and utilisation of machinery for voluntary negotiation between employers or employers' organisations and workers' organisations, with a view to the regulation of terms and conditions of employment by means of collective agreements.

PART X.   FREEDOM OF ASSOCIATION

Article 62

Workers and employers, without distinction whatsoever, shall have the right to establish and, subject only to the rules of the organisation concerned, to join organisations of their own choosing without previous authorisation.

Article 63

1. Workers' and employers' organisations shall have the right to draw up their constitutions and rules, to elect their representatives in full freedom, to organise their administration and activities and to formulate their programmes.

2. The public authorities shall refrain from any interference which would restrict this right or impede the lawful exercise thereof.

Article 64

Workers' and employers' organisations shall not be liable to be dissolved or suspended by administrative authority.

Article 65

Workers' and employers' organisations shall have the right to establish and join federations and confederations and any such organisation, federation or confederation shall have the right to affiliate with international organisations of workers and employers.

Article 66

The provisions of Articles 62, 63 and 64 apply to federations and confederations of workers' and employers' organisations.

Article 67

The acquisition of legal personality by workers' and employers' organisations, federations and confederations shall not be made subject to conditions of such a character as to restrict the application of the provisions of Articles 62, 63 and 64.

Article 68

1. In exercising the rights provided for in this Part of this Convention workers and employers and their respective organisations, like other persons or organised collectivities, shall respect the law of the land.

2. The law of the land shall not be such as to impair, nor shall it be so applied as to impair, the guarantees provided for in this Part of this Convention.

Article 69

In this Part of this Convention the term "organisation" means any organisation of workers or of employers for furthering and defending the interests of workers or of employers.

Article 70

Each Member for which this Part of this Convention is in force undertakes to take all necessary and appropriate measures to ensure that workers and employers may exercise freely the right to organise.

Part XI. Labour Inspection

Article 71

Each Member for which this Convention is in force shall maintain a system of labour inspection.

Article 72

Labour inspection services shall consist of suitably trained inspectors.

Article 73

Workers and their representatives shall be afforded every facility for communicating freely with the inspectors.

Article 74

1. The functions of the system of labour inspection shall be—

(a) to secure the enforcement of the legal provisions relating to conditions of work and the protection of workers while engaged in their work, such as provisions relating to hours, wages, safety, health and welfare, the employment of children and young persons, and other connected matters, in so far as such provisions are enforceable by labour inspectors;

(b) to supply technical information and advice to employers and workers concerning the most effective means of complying with the legal provisions;

(c) to bring to the notice of the competent authority defects or abuses not specifically covered by existing legal provisions.

2. Any further duties which may be entrusted to labour inspectors shall not be such as to interfere with the effective discharge of their primary duties or to prejudice in any way the authority and impartiality which are necessary to inspectors in their relations with employers and workers.

Article 75

The competent authority shall make appropriate arrangements to promote—

(a) effective co-operation between the inspection services and other government services and public or private institutions engaged in similar activities; and

(b) collaboration between officials of the labour inspectorate and employers and workers or their organisations.

Article 76

The inspection staff shall be composed of public officials whose status and conditions of service are such that they are assured of stability of employment and are independent of changes of government and of improper external influences.

Article 77

1. The competent authority shall make the necessary arrangements to furnish labour inspectors with—

(a) local offices, suitably equipped in accordance with the requirements of the service, and accessible to all persons concerned;

(b) the transport facilities necessary for the performance of their duties in cases where suitable public facilities do not exist.

2. The competent authority shall make the necessary arrangements to reimburse to labour inspectors any travelling and incidental expenses which may be necessary for the performance of their duties.

Article 78

1. Labour inspectors provided with proper credentials shall be empowered—

(a) to enter freely and without previous notice at any hour of the day or night any place of employment liable to inspection;

(b) to enter by day any premises which they may have reasonable cause to believe to be liable to inspection; and

(c) to carry out any examination, test or inquiry which they may consider necessary in order to satisfy themselves that the legal provisions are being strictly observed and, in particular—

(i) to interrogate, alone or in the presence of witnesses, the employer or the staff of the undertaking on any matters concerning the application of the legal provisions;

(ii) to require the production of any books, registers or other documents the keeping of which is prescribed by national laws or regulations relating to conditions of work, in order to see that they are in conformity with the legal provisions and to copy such documents or make extracts from them;

(iii) to enforce the posting of notices required by the legal provisions;

(iv) to take or remove for purposes of analysis samples of materials and substances used or handled, subject to the employer or his representative being notified of any samples or substances taken or removed for such purpose.

2. On the occasion of an inspection visit inspectors shall notify the employer or his representative of their presence, unless they consider that such a notification may be prejudicial to the performance of their duties.

Article 79

Subject to such exceptions as may be made by law or regulation, labour inspectors—

(a) shall be prohibited from having any direct or indirect interest in the undertakings under their supervision;

(b) shall be bound on pain of appropriate penalties or disciplinary measures not to reveal, even after leaving the service, any manufacturing or commercial secrets or working processes which may come to their knowledge in the course of their duties; and

(c) shall treat as absolutely confidential the source of any complaint bringing to their notice a defect or breach of legal provisions and shall give no intimation to the employer or his representative that a visit of inspection was made in consequence of the receipt of such a complaint.

Article 80

The labour inspectorate shall be notified of industrial accidents and cases of occupational disease in such cases and in such manner as may be prescribed by national laws or regulations.

Article 81

Places of employment shall be inspected as often and as thoroughly as is necessary to ensure the effective application of the relevant legal provisions.

Article 82

1. Persons who violate or neglect to observe legal provisions enforceable by labour inspectors shall be liable to prompt legal proceedings without previous warning: Provided that exceptions may be made by national laws or regulations in respect of cases in which previous notice to carry out remedial or preventive measures is to be given.

2. It shall be left to the discretion of labour inspectors to give warning and advice instead of instituting or recommending proceedings.

Article 83

Adequate penalties for violations of the legal provisions enforceable by labour inspectors and for obstructing labour inspectors in the performance of their duties shall be provided for by national laws or regulations and effectively enforced.

Article 84

1. Labour inspectors or local inspection offices, as the case may be, shall be required to submit to the central inspection authority periodical reports on the results of their inspection activities.

2. These reports shall be drawn up in such manner and deal with such subjects as may from time to time be prescribed by the central authority; they shall be submitted at least as frequently as may be prescribed by that authority and in any case not less frequently than once a year.

PART XII. HOUSING

Article 85

The appropriate authorities shall, in consultation with the representatives of the employers' and workers' organisations concerned, where such exist, encourage the provision of adequate housing accommodation for plantation workers.

Article 86

1. The minimum standards and specifications of the accommodation to be provided in accordance with the preceding Article shall be laid down by the appropriate public authority. The latter shall, wherever practicable, constitute advisory boards consisting of representatives of employers and workers for consultation in regard to matters connected with housing.

2. Such minimum standards shall include specifications concerning—

(a) the construction materials to be used;

(b) the minimum size of accommodation, its layout, ventilation, and floor and air space;

(c) verandah space, cooking, washing, storage, water supply and sanitary facilities.

Article 87

Adequate penalties for violations of the legal provisions made in accordance with the preceding Article shall be provided for by laws or regulations and effectively enforced.

Article 88

1. Where housing is provided by the employer the conditions under which plantation workers are entitled to occupancy shall be not less favourable than those established by national custom or national legislation.

2. Whenever a resident worker is discharged he shall be allowed a reasonable time in which to vacate the house. Where the time allowed is not fixed by law it shall be determined by recognised negotiating machinery, or, failing agreement on the subject, by recourse to the normal procedure of the civil courts.

PART XIII. MEDICAL CARE

Article 89

The appropriate authorities shall, in consultation with the representatives of the employers' and workers' organisations concerned, where such exist, encourage the provision of adequate medical services for plantation workers and members of their families.

Article 90

1. Medical services shall be of a standard prescribed by the public authorities, shall be adequate having regard to the number of persons involved, and shall be operated by a sufficient number of qualified personnel.

2. Such services where provided by the appropriate public authorities shall conform to the standards, customs and practices of the authority concerned.

Article 91

The appropriate authority, in consultation with the representatives of the employers' and workers' organisations concerned, where such exist, shall take steps in plantation areas to eradicate or control prevalent endemic diseases.

. . . .

Convention No. 141

*Convention concerning Organisations of Rural Workers and
Their Role in Economic and Social Development*

The General Conference of the International Labour Organisation,

Having been convened at Geneva by the Governing Body of the International Labour Office, and having met in its Sixtieth Session on 4 June 1975, and

Recognising that the importance of rural workers in the world makes it urgent to associate them with economic and social development action if their conditions of work and life are to be permanently and effectively improved, and

Noting that in many countries of the world and particularly in developing countries there is massive under-utilisation of land and labour and that this makes it imperative for rural workers to be given every encouragement to develop free and viable organisations capable of protecting and furthering the interests of their members and ensuring their effective contribution to economic and social development, and

Considering that such organisations can and should contribute to the alleviation of the persistent scarcity of food products in various regions of the world, and

Recognising that land reform is in many developing countries an essential factor in the improvement of the conditions of work and life of rural workers and that organisations of such workers should accordingly co-operate and participate actively in the implementation of such reform, and

Recalling the terms of existing international labour Conventions and Recommendations—in particular the Right of Association (Agriculture) Convention, 1921, the Freedom of Association and Protection of the Right to Organise Convention, 1948, and the Right to Organise and Collective Bargaining Convention, 1949—which affirm the right of all workers, including rural workers, to establish free and independent organisations, and the provisions of numerous international labour Conventions and Recommendations applicable to rural workers which call for the participation, inter alia, of workers' organisations in their implementation, and

Noting the joint concern of the United Nations and the specialised agencies, in particular the International Labour Organisation and the Food and Agriculture Organisation of the United Nations, with land reform and rural development, and

Noting that the following standards have been framed in co-operation with the Food and Agriculture Organisation of the United Nations and that, with a view to avoiding duplication, there will be continuing co-operation with that Organisation and with the United Nations in promoting and securing the application of these standards, and

Having decided upon the adoption of certain proposals with regard to organisations of rural workers and their role in economic and social development, which is the fourth item on the agenda of the session, and

Having determined that these proposals shall take the form of an international Convention,

adopts this twenty-third day of June of the year one thousand nine hundred and seventy-five the following Convention, which may be cited as the Rural Workers' Organisations Convention, 1975:

Article 1

This Convention applies to all types of organisations of rural workers, including organisations not restricted to but representative of rural workers.

Article 2

1. For the purposes of this Convention, the term "rural workers" means any person engaged in agriculture, handicrafts or a related occupation in a rural area, whether as a wage earner or, subject to the provisions of paragraph 2 of this Article, as a self-employed person such as a tenant, sharecropper or small owner-occupier.

2. This Convention applies only to those tenants, sharecroppers or small owner-occupiers who derive their main income from agriculture, who work the land themselves, with the help only of their family or with the help of occasional outside labour and who do not—

(a) permanently employ workers; or

(b) employ a substantial number of seasonal workers; or

(c) have any land cultivated by sharecroppers or tenants.

Article 3

1. All categories of rural workers, whether they are wage earners or self-employed, shall have the right to establish and, subject only to the rules of the organisation concerned, to join organisations of their own choosing without previous authorisation.

2. The principles of freedom of association shall be fully respected; rural workers' organisations shall be independent and voluntary in character and shall remain free from all interference, coercion or repression.

3. The acquisition of legal personality by organisations of rural workers shall not be made subject to conditions of such a character as to restrict the application of the provisions of the preceding paragraphs of this Article.

4. In exercising the rights provided for in this Article rural workers and their respective organisations, like other persons or organised collectivities, shall respect the law of the land.

5. The law of the land shall not be such as to impair, nor shall it be so applied as to impair, the guarantees provided for in this Article.

Article 4

It shall be an objective of national policy concerning rural development to facilitate the establishment and growth, on a voluntary basis, of strong and independent organisations of rural workers as an effective means of ensuring the participation of rural workers, without discrimination as defined in the Discrimination (Employment and Occupation) Convention, 1958, in economic and social development and in the benefits resulting therefrom.

Article 5

1. In order to enable organisations of rural workers to play their role in economic and social development, each Member which ratifies this Convention shall adopt and carry out a policy of active encouragement to these organisations, particularly with a view to eliminating obstacles to their establishment, their growth and the pursuit of their lawful activities, as well as such legislative and administrative discrimination against rural workers' organisations and their members as may exist.

2. Each Member which ratifies this Convention shall ensure that national laws or regulations do not, given the special circumstances of the rural sector, inhibit the establishment and growth of rural workers' organisations.

Article 6

Steps shall be taken to promote the widest possible understanding of the need to further the development of rural workers' organisations and of the contribution they can make to improving employment opportunities and general conditions of work and life in rural areas as well as to increasing the national income and achieving a better distribution thereof.

. . . .

Recommendation No. 149

Recommendation concerning Organisations of Rural Workers and Their Role in Economic and Social Development

The General Conference of the International Labour Organisation,

Having been convened at Geneva by the Governing Body of the International Labour Office, and having met in its Sixtieth Session on 4 June 1975, and

Recognising that the importance of rural workers in the world makes it urgent to associate them with economic and social development action if their conditions of work and life are to be permanently and effectively improved, and

Noting that in many countries of the world and particularly in developing countries there is massive under-utilisation of land and labour and that this makes it imperative for rural workers to be given every encouragement to develop free and viable organisations capable of protecting and furthering the interests of their members and ensuring their effective contribution to economic and social development, and

Considering that such organisations can and should contribute to the alleviation of the persistent scarcity of food products in various regions of the world, and

Recognising that land reform is in many developing countries an essential factor in the improvement of the conditions of work and life of rural workers and that organisations of such workers should accordingly co-operate and participate actively in the implementation of such reform, and

Recalling the terms of existing international labour Conventions and Recommendations—in particular the Right of Association (Agriculture) Convention, 1921, the Freedom of Association and Protection of the Right to Organise Convention, 1948, and the Right to Organise and Collective Bargaining Convention, 1949—which affirm the right of all workers, including rural workers, to establish free and independent organisations, and the provisions of numerous international labour Conventions and Recommendations applicable to rural workers which call for the participation, inter alia, of workers' organisations in their implementation, and

Noting the joint concern of the United Nations and the specialised agencies, in particular the International Labour Organisation and the Food and Agriculture Organisation of the United Nations, with land reform and rural development, and

Noting that the following standards have been framed in co-operation with the Food and Agriculture Organisation of the United Nations and that, with a view to avoiding duplication, there will be continuing co-operation with that Organisation and with the United Nations in promoting and securing the application of these standards, and

Having decided upon the adoption of certain proposals with regard to organisations of rural workers and their role in economic and social development, which is the fourth item on the agenda of the session, and

Having determined that these proposals shall take the form of a Recommendation,

adopts this twenty-third day of June of the year one thousand nine hundred and seventy-five the following Recommendation, which may be cited as the Rural Workers' Organisations Recommendation, 1975:

I.   GENERAL PROVISIONS

1. (1) This Recommendation applies to all types of organisations of rural workers, including organisations not restricted to but representative of rural workers.

(2) The Co-operatives (Developing Countries) Recommendation, 1966, further remains applicable to the organisations of rural workers falling within its scope.

2. (1) For the purposes of this Recommendation, the term "rural workers" means any person engaged in agriculture, handicrafts or a related occupation in a rural area, whether as a wage earner or, subject to the provisions of subparagraph (2) of this Paragraph, as a self-employed person such as a tenant, sharecropper or small owner-occupier.

(2) This Recommendation applies only to those tenants, sharecroppers or small owner-occupiers who derive their main income from agriculture, who work the land themselves, with the help only of their family or with the help of occasional outside labour and who do not—

(a) permanently employ workers; or

(b) employ a substantial number of seasonal workers; or

(c) have any land cultivated by sharecroppers or tenants.

3. All categories of rural workers, whether they are wage earners or self-employed, should have the right to establish and, subject only to the rules of the organisation concerned, to join organisations of their own choosing without previous authorisation.

II.   ROLE OF ORGANISATIONS OF RURAL WORKERS

4. It should be an objective of national policy concerning rural development to facilitate the establishment and growth, on a voluntary basis, of strong and independent organisations of rural workers as an effective means of ensuring the participation of rural workers, without discrimination as defined in the Discrimination (Employment and Occupation) Convention, 1958, in economic and social development and in the benefits resulting therefrom.

5. Such organisations should, as appropriate, be able to—

(a) represent, further and defend the interests of rural workers, for instance by undertaking negotiations and consultations at all levels on behalf of such workers collectively;

(b) represent rural workers in connection with the formulation, implementation and evaluation of programmes of rural development and at all stages and levels of national planning;

(c) involve the various categories of rural workers, according to the interests of each, actively and from the outset in the implementation of—

(i) programmes of agricultural development, including the improvement of techniques of production, storing, processing, transport and marketing;

    (ii) programmes of agrarian reform, land settlement and land development;

    (iii) programmes concerning public works, rural industries and rural crafts;

    (iv) rural development programmes, including those implemented with the collaboration of the United Nations, the International Labour Organisation and other specialised agencies;

    (v) the information and education programmes and other activities referred to in Paragraph 15 of this Recommendation:

(d) promote and obtain access of rural workers to services such as credit, supply, marketing and transport as well as to technological services;

(e) play an active part in the improvement of general and vocational education and training in rural areas as well as in training for community development, training for co-operative and other activities of rural workers' organisations and training for the management thereof;

(f) contribute to the improvement of the conditions of work and life of rural workers, including occupational safety and health;

(g) promote the extension of social security and basic social services in such fields as housing, health and recreation.

III.   Means of Encouraging the Growth of Organisations of Rural Workers

6. In order to enable organisations of rural workers to play their role in economic and social development, member States should adopt and carry out a policy of active encouragement to these organisations, particularly with a view to—

(a) eliminating obstacles to their establishment, their growth and the pursuit of their lawful activities, as well as such legislative and administrative discrimination against rural workers' organisations and their members as may exist;

(b) extending to rural workers' organisations and their members such facilities for vocational education and training as are available to other workers' organisations and their members; and

(c) enabling rural workers' organisations to pursue a policy to ensure that social and economic protection and benefits corresponding to those made available to industrial workers or, as appropriate, workers engaged in other non-industrial occupations are also extended to their members.

7. (1) The principles of freedom of association should be fully respected; rural workers' organisations should be independent and voluntary in character and should remain free from all interference, coercion or repression.

(2) The acquisition of legal personality by organisations of rural workers should not be made subject to conditions of such a character as to restrict the application of the provisions of Paragraph 3 and subparagraph (1) of this Paragraph.

(3) In exercising the rights which they enjoy in pursuance of Paragraph 3 and of this Paragraph rural workers and their respective organisations, like other persons or organised collectivities, should respect the law of the land.

(4) The law of the land should not be such as to impair, nor should it be so applied as to impair, the guarantees provided for in Paragraph 3 and in this Paragraph.

A. *Legislative and Administrative Measures*

8. (1) Member States should ensure that national laws or regulations do not, given the special circumstances of the rural sector, inhibit the establishment and growth of rural workers' organisations.

(2) In particular—

(a) the principles of right of association and of collective bargaining, in conformity especially with the Right of Association (Agriculture) Convention, 1921, the Freedom of Association and Protection of the Right to Organise Convention, 1948, and the Right to Organise and Collective Bargaining Convention, 1949, should be made fully effective by the application to the rural sector of general laws or regulations on the subject, or by the adoption of special laws or regulations, full account being taken of the needs of all categories of rural workers;

(b) relevant laws and regulations should be fully adapted to the special needs of rural areas; for instance—

   (i) requirements regarding minimum membership, minimum levels of education and minimum funds should not be permitted to impede the development of organisations in rural areas where the population is scattered, ill educated and poor;

   (ii) problems which may arise concerning the access of organisations of rural workers to their members should be dealt with in a manner respecting the rights of all concerned and in accordance with the terms of the Freedom of Association and Protection of the Right to Organise Convention, 1948, and the Workers' Representatives Convention, 1971;

   (iii) there should be effective protection of the rural workers concerned against dismissal and against eviction which are based on their status or activities as leaders or members of rural workers' organisations.

9. There should be adequate machinery, whether in the form of labour inspection or of special services, or in some other form, to ensure the effective implementation of laws and regulations concerning rural workers' organisations and their membership.

10. (1) Where rural workers find it difficult, under existing conditions, to take the initiative in establishing and operating their own organisations, existing organisations should be encouraged to give them, at their request, appropriate guidance and assistance corresponding to their interests.

(2) Where necessary, such assistance could on request be supplemented by advisory services staffed by persons qualified to give legal and technical advice and to run educational courses.

11. Appropriate measures should be taken to ensure that there is effective consultation and dialogue with rural workers' organisations on all matters relating to conditions of work and life in rural areas.

12. (1) In connection with the formulation and, as appropriate, the application of economic and social plans and programmes and any other general measures concerning the economic, social or cultural development of rural areas, rural workers' organisations should be associated with planning procedures and institutions, such as statutory boards and committees, development agencies and economic and social councils.

(2) In particular, appropriate measures should be taken to make possible the effective participation of such organisations in the formulation, implementation and evaluation of agrarian reform programmes.

13. Member States should encourage the establishment of procedures and institutions which foster contacts between rural workers' organisations, employers and their organisations and the competent authorities.

B. *Public Information*

14. Steps should be taken, particularly by the competent authority, to promote—

(a) the understanding of those directly concerned, such as central, local and other

authorities, rural employers and landlords, of the contribution which can be made by rural workers' organisations to the increase and better distribution of national income, to the increase of productive and remunerative employment opportunities in the rural sector, to the raising of the general level of education and training of the various categories of rural workers and to the improvement of the general conditions of work and life in rural areas;

(b) the understanding of the general public, including, in particular, that in the non-rural sectors of the economy, of the importance of maintaining a proper balance between the development of rural and urban areas, and of the desirability, as a contribution towards ensuring that balance, of furthering the development their rural workers' organisations.

15. These steps might include—

(a) mass information and education campaigns, especially with a view to giving rural workers full and practical information on their rights, so that they may exercise them as necessary;

(b) radio, television and cinema programmes, and periodic articles in the local and national press, describing the conditions of life and work in rural areas and explaining the aims of rural workers' organisations and the results obtained by their activities;

(c) the organisation, locally, of seminars and meetings with the participation of representatives of the various categories of rural workers, of employers and landlords, of other sectors of the population and of local authorities;

(d) the organisation of visits to rural areas of journalists, representatives of employers and workers in industry or commerce, students of universities and schools accompanied by their teachers, and other representatives of the various sectors of the population;

(e) the preparation of suitable curricula for the various types and levels of schools appropriately reflecting the problems of agricultural production and the life of rural workers.

C. *Education and Training*

16. In order to ensure a sound growth of rural workers' organisations and the rapid assumption of their full role in economic and social development, steps should be taken, by the competent authority among others, to—

(a) impart to the leaders and members of rural workers' organisations knowledge of—

   (i) national laws and regulations and international standards on questions of direct concern to the activity of the organisations, in particular the right of association;

   (ii) the basic principles of the establishment and operation of organisations of rural workers;

   (iii) questions regarding rural development as part of the economic and social development of the country, including agricultural and handicraft production, storing, processing, transport, marketing and trade;

   (iv) principles and techniques of national planning at different levels;

   (v) training manuals and programmes which are published or established by the United Nations, the International Labour Organisation or other specialised agencies and which are designed for the education and training of rural workers;

(b) improve and foster the education of rural workers in general, technical, economic and social fields, so as to make them better able both to develop their organisations and understand their rights and to participate actively in rural development; particular attention should be paid to the training of wholly or partly illiterate workers through literacy programmes linked with the practical expansion of their activities;

(c) promote programmes directed to the role which women can and should play in the rural community, integrated in general programmes of education and training to which women and men should have equal opportunities of access;

(d) provide training designed particularly for educators of rural workers, to enable them, for example, to help in the development of co-operative and other appropriate forms of servicing activities which would enable organisations to respond directly to membership needs while fostering their independence through economic self-reliance;

(e) give support to programmes for the promotion of rural youth in general.

17. (1) As an effective means of providing the training and education referred to in Paragraph 16, programmes of workers' education or adult education, specially adapted to national and local conditions and to the social, economic and cultural needs of the various categories of rural workers, including the special needs of women and young persons, should be formulated and applied.

(2) In view of their special knowledge and experience in these fields, trade union movements and existing organisations which represent rural workers might be closely associated with the formulation and carrying out of such programmes.

D. *Financial and Material Assistance*

18. (1) Where, particularly in the initial stages of development, rural workers' organisations consider that they need financial or material assistance, for instance to help them in carrying out programmes of education and training, and where they seek and obtain such assistance, they should receive it in a manner which fully respects their independence and interests and those of their members. Such assistance should be supplementary to the initiative and efforts of rural workers in financing their own organisations.

(2) The foregoing principles apply in all cases of financial and material assistance, including those in which it is the policy of a member State to render such assistance itself.